The Irish Bride's Su

'I could quite honestly spend all day telling you how brilliant this book is, but what I will say is - go and buy it ... NOW!'
www.simplyweddings.com

'This book is to become the wedding bible to all those couples on the path to marriage.'
Sunday World

'An invaluable tool for brides to be.'
Irish Daily Star

'Whether you're tearing your hair out over feuding relatives, dresses that look like meringues or the expense of ice sculptures, or if you're just looking forward to a fun day out with the family and loved ones, then this book should be perfect for you.'
Evening Echo

'From the proposal to sending out thank-you cards, Mac a'Bháird guides the Irish bride through the essentials as well as the wild possibilities open to them.'
Irish Examiner

Natasha Mac a'Bháird grew up in Letterkenny, County Donegal, and later moved to Dublin where she studied history and politics in Trinity College. She returned to Letterkenny for her (perfectly planned) wedding to sports journalist Aidan Fitzmaurice in June 2003. Natasha now lives in Dublin and works in the publishing industry. She is trying not to become a Smug Married. This is her first book.

The
IRISH
BRIDE'S
SURVIVAL GUIDE

PLAN YOUR PERFECT WEDDING

Natasha Mac a'Bháird

THE O'BRIEN PRESS
DUBLIN

First published 2005 by The O'Brien Press Ltd.,
20 Victoria Road, Dublin 6,
Ireland.
Tel: +353 1 4923333; Fax: +353 1 4922777
E-mail: books@obrien.ie
Website: www.obrien.ie
Reprinted 2005.

ISBN: 0-86278-904-4

British Library Cataloguing-in-Publication Data
Mac a'Bháird, Natasha
The Irish bride's survival guide: plan your perfect wedding
1. Weddings - Ireland -Planning
2. Wedding etiquette - Ireland
I.Title
395.2'2'09415

2 3 4 5 6 7 8

05 06 07 08 09

Illustrations: Eva Byrne, pages 46,57,74,116,117,141,146,157,173,194,195,
205,212,217,239,249,267,283
Illustrations: Emma Byrne, pages 11,27,47,75,95,207,226,251,282

Typesetting, editing, layout and design: The O'Brien Press Ltd
Printing: Creative Print and Design

Dedication

To Aidan, for making our wedding day just the first of
the happiest days of my life.

Acknowledgements

Thank you to my wonderful parents, Anne and Conall, and to Áine, Lochlann and Killian, for always believing I would write a book one day.

Thanks to all the brides and grooms who shared their experiences with me and gave me a much greater insight into the world of weddings. Special thanks to 'the Crazies' – Alvina, Anita, Aoife, Caitriona, Céara, Chris, Janet, Lily, Máirín, Paula, Susan and Wendy – we planned our weddings together and you were so supportive during the writing of this book, always ready to offer advice and never afraid to criticise. I hope we'll still be friends when it comes to planning our golden wedding anniversaries.

My gratitude to all the professionals who were so helpful in advising on the finer details, especially the General Register Office and the various church bodies.

Thanks to everyone at O'Brien Press for your belief in and enthusiasm for this book from day one. Thanks to Emma Byrne, who did a wonderful job on the design. Thanks to Ruth and Colm for all your great ideas. Above all, thanks to my editor, Mary Webb, for your inspired suggestions, meticulous checking of details, and constant good humour – you made the whole editing process (supposed to be a nightmare) actually fun.

Finally, thanks to my beloved husband Aidan – not only did you contribute your own chapter, you read every word I wrote before I dared to show anyone else. And despite secretly thinking that all brides (especially me) are slightly mad, you were always so encouraging and supportive. Thank you for everything.

Contents

Introduction

Congratulations on your engagement! Your head is probably filled with dreams of gorgeous white dresses, five-tiered wedding cakes, and your handsome fiancé waiting for you as you walk down the aisle. But soon you'll have lost all sense of proportion, and be wondering if the napkins the hotel have suggested match the bridesmaid's dress exactly, did your mother really mean it when she said she'd invited your ex-boyfriend, and can a tiara possibly make you look fat?

Welcome to the weird and wonderful world of weddings. It's a place which turns normal, rational women into hysterical Bridezillas obsessed with every tiny detail. But don't worry – it doesn't have to be that way. Your wedding plans will spiral out of control only if you let them. Keep your sense of humour – and your common sense – intact. And remember, that important though it is, your wedding day is just one day, but your marriage is for life.

Organising a wedding can be a very daunting task. There are so many things to think about and decisions to be made, and sometimes you simply don't know where to start.

One thing you will find out very quickly is that planning a wedding is a lesson in assertiveness. Everyone has an opinion on so many aspects of weddings, and most people won't hesitate to tell you what they think you should be doing. Don't let yourself be bullied into decisions you're not happy with. Discuss the issues with your fiancé and make the choice that's right for you as a couple. It's your day, and no-one else should be allowed to dictate what you can and can't do.

Above all, make sure you enjoy the planning process. It'll all be over before you know it, and you'll wish you could do it all over again.

When I was planning my wedding I would have loved a book that told me all I needed to know, so, once the madness of wedding planning was over, I decided to write my own (just when my husband thought he could finally throw out my stack of wedding magazines). I have written this book based on my experience of organising a wedding and the dozens of tips I picked up along the way. I also talked to lots of former brides and grooms about their weddings, so this book is the result of many people's experiences. I hope you'll find it helpful in planning your day.

Your wedding day is supposed to be the best day of your life. Hopefully this book will help you make sure that it is.

CHAPTER ONE

Rules of Engagement

THE PROPOSAL

I won't dwell too long on the proposal, as if you've bought this book, we can assume it has already taken place. (If not, then you may have some problems I can't help you with). However, since the proposal is the spark that ignites the raging inferno of wedding plans that will quickly take over your life, it would be rude not to mention it. Also, and I think it fair to warn you about this now, the proposal may be the only scene in this play in which your man plays the leading role. Unless you have landed a truly exceptional fellow, your new fiancé is likely to assume that having popped the question, his next job will be to get to the church on time.

Ideally, your proposal should be all you've ever dreamed of. It's a gloriously sunny/dramatically stormy/romantically snowy day, your Prince Charming whisks you off to a beautiful countryside setting/your favourite restaurant/the top of the Eiffel Tower, makes a moving speech about how much you mean to him, drops to one knee and produces a rock to rival the iceberg that hit the Titanic.

Chris, Dublin

We were living in New Zealand, my fiancé's home country. He took me away for the weekend on the devious premise that he had to check out the conference facilities for work. I had no idea what he had planned! He chose a resort in the Far North because it is the closest point to Ireland and he knew I was missing home. He had the ring, which he'd had designed specially, tucked away in his pocket, and a bottle of champagne chilling in the back of the car. I was getting real fidgety, so he thought I knew what he was up to and that I was feeling nervous. He suddenly said, literally as one word, 'Are-you-really-nervous-will-you-marry-me?' I hadn't had time to digest his first question when his second suddenly hit me ... like a steamroller! I was completely shocked, but managed to say yes! We toasted our engagement sitting on a bench overlooking the Tasman Sea.

But sometimes the reality can be less than ideal.

Claire, Wexford

Most proposal stories are so romantic – mine is just the opposite. All our friends were getting engaged and kept asking why we weren't, but I am just not that corny – or so I thought! We went out to buy some furniture for our sitting room and spent hours disagreeing in large superstores, and eventually went home, very cranky and without the furniture!

We were sitting in front of the TV with a Chinese takeaway, and I don't know if it was the money burning a hole in his pocket, but somehow he suggested that as we did not get the furniture and had the money we 'may as well' buy an engagement ring instead! I laughed and said yes.

As we live in the UK, we called Ireland with the good news and missed the best engagement party in history, which was held there and then without us! Mam still says it was the worst hangover of her life.

If your proposal didn't live up to your romantic fantasy, don't dwell on it. You are marrying the man of your dreams and that's what matters – even if your dreams have changed somewhat over the years. Move on, in the comfortable knowledge that at least your wedding day will be perfect, because *you* are in charge of planning that.

Tired of waiting? The DIY proposal

We may be modern girls but most of us would hate the idea of being the one to propose. And since, as I may have mentioned earlier, the guy's helpfulness with the rest of the wedding preparations is generally minimal, it's not too much to ask that he set the ball rolling. But if you're sick and tired of waiting for him to screw up the courage, then go for it. Traditionally, women are allowed to propose during a leap year, but there's nothing to stop you doing it any old time you feel like it.

So, in case you've bought this book in advance of The Proposal and are planning to surprise your man, please be sure to hide it in a very safe place until he's said yes, or you risk a boyfriend-shaped hole in your front door as he runs for his life.

THE RING

Tradition

The engagement ring acquired its significance in AD860, when Pope Nicholas I decreed that an aspiring bridegroom should present his fiancée with a ring of gold as proof that his intentions were genuine. Diamonds came into fashion after King Maximilian of Hapsburg gave Mary of Burgundy a diamond engagement ring in 1477. Diamonds are the most enduring substance in nature, so they represent the permanence of the commitment.

The tradition of wearing engagement and wedding rings on the third finger of the left hand originated with the ancient Romans, who believed that there was a vein in that finger which was directly connected to the heart. However, in some other European countries, the wedding ring is worn on the third finger of the right hand.

Choosing the ring

Only the very traditional, extremely brave or downright foolish suitor will buy the engagement ring without first consulting his bride-to-be. If your fiancé has done so, chances are you will love it because of the time and thought he has taken to choose it for you. If you really hate it, however, you need to make a decision.

Will your new fiancé be devastated if you admit you don't like the ring and want to exchange it? Could you grow to love the ring in time, like that stray puppy you didn't want to adopt? Or is its presence on your finger going to be a constant cause of frustration and disappointment to you? If so, talk to your fiancé now. He wants you to be happy, and after all, it's you who's going to have to wear the damn thing.

While it may not conform to the fairytale scenario, it's far easier to choose the ring together. Some would even say it's more romantic, especially if you make a day of it. Arrange to go for lunch and have a glass of champagne to celebrate a successful purchase.

When selecting your engagement ring, don't forget to think about your wedding ring also, and how they will sit together. Both rings should be made of the same type of metal – yellow gold, white gold, platinum – and also of the same carat, otherwise the softer metal could be worn down by the other. If your engagement ring is an unusual shape, you may have to get a wedding ring specially made to match it. Check with the jeweller when you buy your engagement ring and see what they suggest.

Diamonds are a girl's best friend

Diamonds are rated on four features: cut, clarity, colour and carat.

Cut is the most important feature. It allows light to move into the stone and reflect outwards, so a well-cut diamond will sparkle the most. Brilliant cut (old and new style), emerald, princess, oval, square, pear and heart-shaped are the most popular.

Clarity refers to the number of tiny flaws or inclusions in the stone. A completely flawless diamond is extremely rare, but the fewer flaws a stone has the more it will sparkle, and the more expensive it will be.

Colour is another feature on which a diamond is judged. The best diamonds are pure white, while less perfect stones will be tinted to a greater or lesser degree.

Carat is the weight of the diamond, and larger diamonds of more than one carat are rare.

Naturally-occuring coloured diamonds – pink, blue, yellow – are very rare, and therefore very expensive. The Hope Diamond, the largest and most famous blue diamond in the world, weighed in at a hefty 45.5 carats. Although beautiful to look at, it was said to bring its owners bad luck, so it now resides in the Smithsonian Institute in Washington.

Celebrity style

Richard Burton presented Elizabeth Taylor with a 69-carat pear-shaped diamond as a token of his affection. The couple married, divorced, re-married and finally split for good. At its last recorded sale in 1979, the Taylor-Burton diamond fetched almost $3,000,000.

Diamonds – whether solitaires, two or three stones, or a whole cluster – remain the most popular engagement stone, but you could also consider your birth stone, either alone or in combination with diamonds:

MONTH	STONE	SYMBOLISING
January	Garnet	Constancy
February	Amethyst	Sincerity
March	Aquamarine	Courage
April	Diamond	Innocence
May	Emerald	Success
June	Pearl	Health
July	Ruby	Contentment
August	Peridot	Happiness
September	Sapphire	Wisdom
October	Opal	Hope
November	Topaz	Fidelity
December	Turquoise	Prosperity

Don't get too bogged down in the details; the most important thing when choosing your ring, diamond or otherwise, is simply that you like it and that it suits your hand. And, as you'll find when you go shopping for your wedding dress, what actually looks good on you may be completely different from what you had in mind originally. Go with your instincts, and you're sure to find a ring you love and which makes you smile every time you glance down at your left hand; the novelty of wearing an engagement ring is a joy that lasts for quite some time.

Other options

You've traipsed around every jewellers in Ireland or even beyond, and you haven't found anything you like – so why not design your own ring? Jewellery designers can help you turn your ideas into a ring that's really unique. Draw a picture of what you have in mind, or bring pictures cut from magazines or printed out from the internet.

The only drawback here is that you'll be committed to buying a ring before you see it, so try to find a designer who's willing to be flexible and who will alter the design until you're happy, without charging you a small fortune.

Another lovely option is to wear a ring that is a family heirloom, if one of you is lucky enough to have such an item. If you don't like the ring itself, you could get the stone reset into a design of your choosing. Alternatively, you could have a ring, or some other piece of jewellery that is special to you, melted down and transformed into a new ring – that way you have the link to your family history but in a ring that's personal to you.

Mary, Co Cork

My mother had inherited a rather pretty but very old-fashioned bar brooch set with a central emerald, flanked by diamonds and seed pearls, which she gave to me when I was twenty-one. It seemed a shame to leave it, unworn, in a drawer, so when I was getting engaged, I had a jeweller take the brooch apart and he designed an engagement ring with four diamonds, a wedding ring set with seven little diamonds in a pavè style and a tear-drop pendant from the emerald. My mother was delighted, I was delighted, and it worked out at a fraction of the cost of buying the rings.

Caring for your ring

You should have your engagement ring cleaned every six to twelve months and have the setting checked at the same time in case any stones have become loose. The jeweller where you bought your ring should provide this service free for life.

Do I *have* to wear an engagement ring?

No you don't, and many modern brides are choosing not to. It's up to the bride to decide if she does or doesn't want to wear a ring, so don't be pressurised into the decision, either by your fiancé or by anyone else. If you're not really into jewellery, you won't want to wear two rings on one finger, so getting an engagement ring could be a bit of a waste. Or you might fall in love with a really distinctive, unusual ring that will be difficult to match with a second ring, in which case you'd be better off saving this to use as your wedding ring. You could, of course,

Kunak, Co Louth

When we got engaged I wasn't sure I wanted an engagement ring, but I did have my heart set on a cello, so I suggested to my fiancé that he get me an 'engagement cello' instead. Needless to say, he wasn't too impressed with the idea, pointing out that it would be quite difficult to lug a cello around to show friends and family the 'expression' of our love, although the money saved on the ring would help cover the costs of the resulting hernia!

move your engagement ring to your right hand after you are married, wearing just the wedding band on your left hand.

Having said all that, people *will* expect you to have a ring and will ask to see it as soon as you tell them you're engaged – so if you decide against one, be prepared for a few raised eyebrows.

What about the groom?

You're getting a beautiful ring to mark your engagement, so maybe you'd like to buy your fiancé a present too. A watch is probably the most popular gift, and fits in nicely with the idea of your engagement ring, as it's something to wear and show off, and hopefully keep forever. Other possibilities might be a digital camera, a DVD player, a leather wallet, or something that can be engraved with the date – a signet ring, hip flask, silver/pewter drinking mug, Cross pen, cufflinks, etc. Apparently there are 'engagement rings' available for men now too – diamond optional.

However, you don't *have* to buy him something (sorry, guys) – it's not actually a tradition, rather something that has evolved in recent years. I'm afraid I'd never heard of the idea when we got engaged so my poor husband got nothing.

ANNOUNCING THE NEWS

Your parents should be the first to hear your good news, unless either of you has children from a previous relationship, in which case it's their right to find out first.

Traditionally, the bride's parents are told first – possibly because the bride's father was expected to pay for the upcoming nuptials, so it was deemed polite to alert him to the forthcoming drain on his finances as early as possible.

Of course, if you are sticking strictly to tradition, your prospective husband should ask your father's permission for your hand in marriage. Now don't all laugh at once. While most grooms baulk at the idea, and most brides object to the notion of themselves as property to be passed from one man to another, there are women – and fathers – out there who like this idea. If you are one of them, talk nicely to your fiancé and explain how much it would mean to you and your father. Persuade him that this is the perfect way to begin his career as favoured son-in-law.

Once you've told both sets of parents, and, hopefully, had a positive reaction, you can set about spreading the news far and wide. This is one of the happiest pieces of news you will ever tell your friends, so make the most of it. Try not to tell people by phone or e-mail – nothing beats seeing the look of shock and delight on their faces. Make sure that those closest to you hear it from you first, and do resort to phoning if there is a risk that they will hear it from someone else.

A fun way to tell everyone at once is to throw a party for no apparent reason. Once everyone is assembled, break open the bubbly and inform your guests that they're there to celebrate your engagement. Then sit back and enjoy the squeals of delight and the experience of being hugged by seventeen people at once. Of course, the downside to this is that you may miss out on a few engagement presents, and you'll have to buy the champagne yourself.

Some people choose a more unconventional method of breaking the news:

Rebecca, Co Meath

My husband has always had a great imagination, so I should have known he wouldn't announce our engagement in the usual way. He had five-piece jigsaws made, and posted one piece a day for a week.

It caused great excitement; our family and friends were checking TV and radio stations to see if there was some kind of prize on offer. The last piece solved the mystery, giving our names and the date of our engagement.

ENGAGEMENT PARTY

If you're dying for an opportunity to show off your sparkler and indulge in a glass or three of champagne, an engagement party is the way to go. Do a quick once-over with a duster and invite people over to celebrate in style. Or hire a room in your local pub and let someone else worry about clearing up the mess.

Most people consider a card enough to give for an engagement, but some will bring presents, so be sure to note who gave what and send thank-you cards. This will be good practice for the wedding. If you're having the party at home, have plenty of vases in stock for the many bunches of flowers you are sure to receive, or you'll end up cutting the tops off Coke bottles to accommodate your expanding forest of lilies, which somewhat spoils the effect.

Engagement parties are a good opportunity to introduce the two sets of parents and siblings if they haven't already met. It's a joyous occasion to celebrate the good fortune of their son and daughter in finding each other, so moods will be good. Any nerves will be calmed after a couple of champagne cocktails or glasses of their favourite tipple. And if the families dislike each other on sight, there will be plenty of other people to talk to instead.

If a party is not for you, then a meal out with family or drinks with friends is just as good a way to mark the occasion. Just be prepared for the fact that *all* of your friends are going to want to celebrate with you in some way. It may be easiest in the long term to celebrate with everyone at once with a big bash.

NEWSPAPER ANNOUNCEMENT

You may like to spread your news as far and wide as possible by putting a notice in the newspaper. The most popular national paper for engagement notices is *The Irish Times*, which prints these on Saturdays on the letters page. And you don't have to have an address on the DART line or a father with an impressive title to announce your engagement there!

Give the advertising department a call and ask about their rates, guidelines on the number of words, and the deadline for submitting the announcement, and get scribbling. *See* examples overleaf.

If you feel it's too late to put in an engagement announcement, why not put in a marriage announcement instead? *See* over.

From the bride's parents:

From the bride and groom:

MARY PINK – JOHN BLUE

David and Anne Pink, Rathrock, Dublin, are delighted to announce the engagement of their (eldest/ second) daughter Mary to John, son of James and Patricia Blue, of Mara, Co. Galway.

MARY PINK – JOHN BLUE

Mary and John, together with their families in Rathrock, Dublin and in Mara, Co. Galway, are delighted to announce their engagement.

From divorced parents making a joint announcement:

From a remarried mother and stepfather:

MARY PINK – JOHN BLUE

David Pink of London, and Anne Pink of Dublin, are delighted to announce the engagement of their daughter Mary to John, son of James and Patricia Blue, of Mara, Co. Galway.

MARY PINK – JOHN BLUE

Anne and Michael Green, Dublin, are delighted to announce the engagement of her daughter, Mary Pink, to John, son of James and Patricia Blue, of Mara, Co. Galway.

Marriage Announcement:

Mary Pink and John Blue, together with their families, are delighted to announce that they were married in Rome on 12 March 2005.

Celebrity style

When Ryan Tubridy got engaged to Anne Marie, the announcement in *The Irish Times* was from their three-year-old daughter Ella.

Becoming a Fiancée

So what is different now that you are engaged? The most obvious change, apart from the satisfying twinkle every time you move your left hand, is that you have been upgraded from boyfriend and girlfriend and now have full permission to call each other fiancé/fiancée. This lets the world know that not only are you lucky enough to have found your soulmate, you're currently in the process of planning the happiest day of your life. Some brides-to-be love the newfound status the use of the phrase 'my fiancé' confers. Others find the term too pretentious – if this sounds like you, feel free to continue saying boyfriend/partner/significant other. You'll have to get used to 'husband' soon enough, and too much change can be confusing.

You will notice a difference in people's attitudes. You'll find they take you more seriously as a couple, and you won't be asked the sort of questions that may have infuriated you in the past. It will now be perfectly obvious that you're not on the lookout for someone better, or that you don't want to go trekking around the Australian outback for six months, leaving your beloved at home.

As far as your parents are concerned, your impending marriage is final proof that their little girl has grown up. You may find that they regard you as more of an equal, and begin to treat your future husband as part of the family, if they didn't already do so.

And how will *you* feel? Well, a new sense of security will certainly take over your relationship. You'll feel free to make plans for the wedding and beyond – maybe for the dream house you will build some day, or whether you would be happy to call a boy Zachariah after his paternal grandfather!

On the other hand, after the first euphoria has subsided somewhat, you may panic that you're too young to be settling down, that you're missing out on the fun of singledom and that there are too many disappointed men out there who never got the opportunity to snog you. You'll probably feel like this while listening to your single friends prepare to hit the town on a Saturday night. Call them on Sunday morning instead, listen to them bemoan the fact that all the good men are taken, and count yourself lucky that you got in there on time. You may be leaving behind one way of life but another, very satisfying one, is just about to begin.

CHAPTER TWO

When? How? Where?

The parents have been told, the friends have screamed with excitement, the bottles of champagne have all been drunk. You've had some time, probably just a few short weeks, to enjoy being a fiancée, with the prospect of happy ever after glittering before you. There's just one small challenge to be overcome – that's right, you have to organise a wedding. You are no longer a fiancée, you are a bride-to-be and have a million and one things to arrange before you walk down that aisle.

Make lists – it helps you feel calm if the jobs you need to do are written down rather than churning around in your head, and it's very satisfying to cross things off when they're done.

27

Have a look at the **Countdown Checklist**, page 284, for the major tasks that need to be done, and set your own rough schedule, depending on how long you have to plan. Get a wedding folder and start filing everything to do with the day – you may feel like a bit of a Bridezilla, but it will save a lot of headaches later on.

WHEN?
CHOOSING A DATE

First things first. You need to sit down with the lucky groom-to-be and set a date. Think about what time of year you'd like to get married. Maybe you're the sort of girl who has dreamt all her life about being a summer bride, stepping out of a Rolls Royce with the sun glistening on yards of white satin, mingling with your guests in a rose garden after the ceremony, your dress trailing behind you over the freshly-mown grass. Then you remember that you live in Ireland and you're just as likely to have sunshine in March as in August.

Perhaps you and your fiancé have never outgrown the magic of Christmas and your idea of a perfect wedding is walking down an aisle decorated with candles and holly berries, coming in from the bracing cold to a glass of mulled wine, and chatting to your guests by an open log fire.

Each season has its advantages and disadvantages, and although summer remains the most popular time to get married, with Christmas a close second, weddings take place all year round and if you want to get married on a rainy Monday in January then that's entirely your choice.

Many couples are now planning their weddings around

where they'd like to go on honeymoon. October is a good time to visit the US and Canada as flights are less expensive, while the weather remains quite pleasant. If you fancy a European honeymoon but don't like the heat and crowds associated with summer, then spring might be your choice.

You could also choose a date that means something to you as a couple, such as your birthday (though this means one present instead of two in years to come), or the day you met.

Aoife, Co Wicklow

We decided to get married in October because we wanted to go to the US on honeymoon and the prices drop dramatically on October 1st! Also, neither of us are great tanners and the heat can get to us after a while, which is why we normally go on holidays in the autumn. We picked New York, Cape Cod and Boston because they are much quieter at this time of year, infinitely more affordable and less crowded than in summer so we can really enjoy the trip.

Sarah, Co Cavan

When we told people we were getting married on Friday the thirteenth, reactions ranged from laughter to outright disbelief. We didn't care as our only associations with that date were good ones – we first met on Friday the thirteenth six years earlier, so the day was very lucky for us. And there was an unexpected bonus to other people's negativity towards that date: we found that there was much greater availability of suppliers, venues etc than there would have been had we picked a popular date.

What about your guests?

Consider how the different times of year will affect your guests. If your wedding is in the summer it may clash with their holidays, although if you give them plenty of notice this is not a very good excuse for them to miss your big day. On the other hand, bad weather in winter may prevent guests from travelling.

Try to take into account significant occasions in the lives of you and your fiancé's immediate families. First Communions in May could keep young families busy, and State exams in June are another disruption. If you have a lot of family or friends living overseas, you may want to pick a date when it's easy for them to travel home, such as Christmas.

It's impossible to suit everyone, but do think about those you most want to be there, or you may be disappointed. Remember too that you'll need lots of help and support from those closest to you in the week before the wedding, so you'll benefit from choosing a time when they don't have other commitments.

Now, you mightn't think of this, but be aware that the sports calendar could significantly impact upon your wedding plans! Within minutes of his beautifully romantic proposal, my new fiancé remarked that we wouldn't be able to get married the following summer as the World Cup was on. He has some excuse since he writes about soccer for a living, but if you, your families or friends are sports-mad it may be worth at least noting the dates of major sportings events, especially if you're getting married in the summer. If you don't want guests dashing out of the reception to check the score or listening to mini radios in the church, try to work around it.

Of course, you can't plan for every eventuality, as fixtures aren't always known in advance. So don't get too hung up on it;

once you've set your date, those who care about you will just
have to put your wedding ahead of watching the last few holes
of the golf classic. It won't kill them for once.

Fionnuala, Dublin

My fiancé and my brother are both huge sports fans, so
despite the fact that I have no interest in sports myself, I had
to make sure I chose a wedding date that fitted in between
Euro 2004 and the Olympics. Thank goodness there wasn't
an unexpected GAA replay on the day.

And, as always, there are some ancient words of supposed
wisdom on wedding months, contained in the following
traditional rhyme:

Married when the year is new, he'll be loving, kind and true.
When February birds do mate, you wed nor dread your fate.
If you wed when March winds blow, joy and sorrow both you'll know.
Marry in April when you can, joy for maiden and for man.
Marry in the month of May, and you'll surely rue the day.
Marry when June roses grow, over land and sea you'll go.
Those who in July do wed, must labour for their daily bread.
Whoever wed in August be, many a change is sure to see.
Marry in September's shrine, your living will be rich and fine.
If in October you do marry, love will come but riches tarry.
If you wed in bleak November, only joys will come, remember.
When December snows fall fast, marry and true love will last.

Despite the rhyme's warning, May is one of the most popular months for weddings, and November one of the least, so I wouldn't worry too much about it. Your choice of date will undoubtedly be influenced by far more practical matters such as the availability of your chosen venue, particularly if you have only a short time to plan.

What Day?

Marry on Monday for health,
Tuesday for wealth,
Wednesday the best day of all,
Thursday for losses,
Friday for crosses,
Saturday no luck at all.

Regardless of this advice, Saturday is still the most popular day for weddings, with Friday a close second. Weekday weddings are definitely worth considering if you're on a budget or indeed if you have a shorter length of time to plan your wedding, as Fridays and Saturdays get booked up well in advance. Many hotels will offer a discount for Monday to Thursday weddings, and some venues which require minimum numbers for weekend weddings will take smaller weddings on weekdays.

However, do take into account that guests may have difficulty getting time off work during the week. The same applies to Fridays, of course, but at least most people will have Saturday off to recover or indeed to travel home. Thursday weddings often see grumpy designated drivers dragging their spouses home at midnight because they need to work the next day.

Celebrity Style

Elizabeth Taylor got married on a Tuesday, Thursday, Friday, Saturday and Sunday, and didn't seem to have too much luck with any of them.

What time should we hold the ceremony?

In Ireland, most wedding ceremonies are held between 12 noon and 4pm. Winter weddings are often held early because the light will start to fade in mid-afternoon, making it more difficult to get good photographs.

There are pros and cons to having a wedding early in the day: the earlier the ceremony, the more time you'll have for the celebrations afterwards, and if you have to vacate the reception venue at a respectable hour, then an early ceremony is definitely better.

On the other hand, you don't want the morning to be a big rush. You'll feel much more relaxed if you have plenty of time for hair and beauty appointments, taking photos and giggling with your bridesmaids. Also remember that guests may be travelling on the morning of the wedding, so give them time – if they have to set off at the crack of dawn, they may be too tired to enjoy the evening reception.

HOW?

WHAT KIND OF WEDDING DO WE WANT?

The next important decision to make is the style of the wedding. Do you want it to be traditional/ formal/ modern/ fun/ stylish/ themed? Will you have the ceremony in a registry office or in church? How many guests do you want/can you afford to ask? Do you want a big bash in a hotel or would you prefer something smaller and more intimate?

You and your fiancé should discuss in detail the kind of wedding you want before you tell anyone else. If you have different ideas, work out a compromise between you. That way you'll both be clear about what you want and will be able to present a united front before you involve other people who may attempt to influence your decisions.

Does size really matter?

You probably have a vague idea of the number of guests you'd like to invite (before you actually sit down to compose the guest list and realise how far out you were). Budget will be a major consideration, but not the only one. Perhaps your dream venue will hold only a small number of guests – or perhaps it will look empty with less than 200. You may be a shy violet who hates the thought of being the centre of attention and wants only her closest friends and family there. Or maybe you won't feel properly married unless the ceremony is witnessed by everyone from your long-lost cousin to your brother's girlfriend's secretary's aunt.

What are the advantages of having a big or small wedding?

With a big wedding:

💗 You won't have to worry about cutting down on your guest list, or risk arguments with both sets of parents about who they can and can't invite

💗 You'll create a real sense of occasion, with you as the celebrity surrounded by all your devoted fans

💗 You won't have to worry that the church/reception venue/dance floor will look empty

💗 The seating plan will be much easier as you will have plenty of 'mix and mingle' choices to ensure that shy/single/problem guests are with a suitable grouping

💗 You'll get lots more presents!

On the other hand, with a small wedding:

💗 You'll create a lovely sense of intimacy, and all your guests will feel very special to be among the chosen few

💗 You'll be able to spend time with each guest

💗 You won't have to buy dinner for people you normally wouldn't even invite over for a cup of tea

💗 You'll be able to afford extra little touches – perhaps a more expensive favour for each guest to remember your day by, a welcome pack for out-of-town guests, or a fireworks display to round off the night.

Lily, Co Donegal

In North Donegal, it is customary to have large weddings and we certainly followed the trend, with 300 guests.

It was very nerve-racking standing at the bottom of the aisle. The number of people in the church was quite overwhelming, especially with so many faces I didn't recognise, as they were guests invited by my husband that I had never even met before.

At the reception, the guests were all waiting for us and gave us a standing ovation as we entered the packed room. It really was the most fabulous feeling in the world. We both felt very special knowing that all these people were there just for us. When the dancing started the floor never emptied and the atmosphere was amazing.

Looking back, I don't think we would have enjoyed a small wedding – having a large party seemed like the perfect way to celebrate our marriage. We also received a huge number of presents, ranging from cash gifts to household items. In fact, the cash presents we received covered most of the wedding expenses.

Smaller weddings can be just as wonderful, as you'll see from more stories in this chapter.

WHERE?
HERE, THERE OR ANYWHERE ...

Most weddings involve two parts: the ceremony and the reception, with different venues for each. It's important to consider the two venues together when making your plans, in terms of availability, suitability for the style of wedding you want, and location. Ideally, there shouldn't be more than an hour's drive between the two.

Think about where you'd like to get married. Many couples still adhere to the tradition of holding the ceremony in the bride's home town, but that may not be practical, particularly if you, and many of your guests, live a long distance from there. Consider other options – perhaps the groom's home town, if it is nearer, the area where you both live now, or somewhere else entirely. Many Dublin couples are choosing to get married in Meath or Wicklow or even beyond the Pale because prices are generally lower outside the city. Do remember, though, that it's much easier to source suppliers and make arrangements if you – or your mother – are living relatively close to the wedding location.

Church or registry office?

At the time of writing, the only two places where a marriage can legally take place in Ireland are the office of a registrar for civil marriages (a registry office) or an approved church ('church' in this context includes synagogues and Society of Friends' [Quaker] Meeting Houses). *See* Chapter 5 for the legal requirements for civil and church weddings and for details of forthcoming changes to these rules, which will broaden the range of venues available.

Despite all the major shifts in Irish society in recent decades, 95% of Irish couples are still choosing to get married in church. However, this situation is likely to change, with the significant increase in the number of second marriages now taking place. It is very difficult for divorcees to marry in church in Ireland, so if yours is a second wedding, it is likely that the ceremony will take place in a registry office. If you are keen to have some church involvement, there are a number of churches where you can have a marriage blessing. (*see* Chapter 5 for more on this)

Even couples who are not regular churchgoers often want to get married in church, and most clergy are fine with this, but you should check with the church in which you intend to get married.

Registry office weddings have the advantage of being much cheaper – you won't need to pay musicians, and flowers are not usually necessary, except a bouquet for the bride. They do mean, though, that the number of guests you can invite to the actual ceremony is much smaller; some hold only around thirty people.

Choosing a church

For many couples the choice is straightforward: they choose the bride's home parish church, or occasionally the groom's, or where they are both living now. However, there could be several reasons why you don't want to do this – perhaps the church is too big for the size of wedding you have in mind, or it's too far from the reception venue you have your heart set on.

It is possible to get married in a church outside your own parish, but you will need to get the permission of the clergy of the church where you want to marry, and often your own clergy as well, who may be aggrieved that you don't want to get married in their church. Sometimes you'll be asked to make a donation to your own church even though you're not using it, on the grounds that weddings of parishioners form part of the funds required for the upkeep of the church.

Choosing a registry office

Unfortunately, as the law currently stands, there's not much choice in the matter of registry offices, as there is only one in each county. If you really don't like your local registry office, or it can't accommodate the number of guests you'd like to invite, consider having the legal part of the marriage only at the registry office, attended just by your witnesses, then a separate ceremony at your reception venue which all your guests can attend. (More on this in Chapter 5.)

How do we choose a reception venue?

Hotels are still the most popular option because they can adapt to cater for various sizes of weddings and can offer services and expertise which mean you have much less to organise yourselves. There is the added advantage that many or all of your guests can stay in the hotel, thus prolonging the celebrations.

If you haven't a dream venue already in mind and plan to look at a large number of hotels, save yourselves some time by ringing first to ask the basic questions: availability of dates and their requirements for minimum and maximum numbers. If these are suitable, ask them to send you out brochures. This should narrow down your search a little.

Some of the points you should consider when checking out a hotel are:

♥ Does it have the right 'feel' that you want for your wedding?

♥ Does it have a good reputation for weddings? Ask around in the locality, and if possible talk to couples who have had their receptions there in the last few years. You could also post a message on one of the Irish wedding websites asking for feedback

♥ How far is it from your church or registry office? Remember to consider traffic if your wedding is in a city

♥ What does the price include? Most hotels will give you a set price per head, which will cover that number of meals and also extras such as the bridal suite on the wedding night, changing facilities for the bridal party, a cake stand, and somewhere to take photos if it rains

♥ Does the hotel cater for more than one wedding on the same day, and if so, how does it keep the two parties separate?

♥ What sort of a menu is offered and how flexible is this? Will you be able to get vegetarian or other alternatives?

♥ Can you use your wedding cake as dessert? Many hotels include dessert in their set menu and price, and won't give you a reduction even if you'd rather just have the cake

♥ Can you supply your own wine and how much is the corkage charge?

♥ Does music have to finish at a set time, or is it possible to get a late licence?

♥ Does the hotel allow 'afters' guests?

♥ What are the rooms like for the guests – and the bridal suite for you?

♥ Is there a special room rate for wedding guests?

♥ Very important: Is any major building work planned for the time of your wedding? (The last thing you want to discover the week of your wedding is that the string quartet will be drowned out by drilling and hammering and that the car park has been transformed into a sea of mud).

If you can, find out when another wedding is taking place in the hotel and have a look at the function room – even if it's just for a quick peek. You'll be able to picture everything so much better when you see tables, chairs, flowers and decorations in place instead of viewing an empty room. It's also a good idea to have lunch or dinner in your preferred hotel so you can check out the quality of the food and taste the house wine.

Extensive hotel grounds and gardens are a lovely bonus. You will be able to have your photographs taken there, and could even hold your drinks reception outside. Guests can wander out for fresh air (or cigarettes!), and if you're inviting children, they can work off some energy by running around outside. However, all this is dependent on the weather, something we can never rely on in Ireland, so don't let this influence you too much – there's no point in having a fabulous outdoor setting if you're stuck in a dingy reception room if it rains.

Other options

For a real fairytale atmosphere, consider one of the many castles around Ireland that cater for weddings. They are not a cheap option, but will certainly make the occasion a memorable one for all your guests – and will make for some truly spectacular photographs. Some castles operate in the same way as hotels, providing the meal, drinks and other services for you, while others will require that you bring in your own caterers.

You will find listings of Irish castle hotels on several internet sites, including www.hotel-ireland.com/castles and www.celticcastles/com, where there is a link to the websites of the individual castles.

Celebrity Style

Paul McCartney and Heather Mills held their wedding reception in Castle Leslie, Co Monaghan; Posh and Becks held theirs in Luttrellstown Castle; Pierce Brosnan and Keely Shaye-Smith got married in Ballytubber Abbey and followed this with a reception in Ashford Castle; Kinnitty Castle in Offaly was the venue for the wedding of Ozzy Osbourne's son Louis to Louise Lennon.

Weddings at home

If you fancy something a bit more personal and are lucky enough to have parents/relatives with a big house or a garden large enough for a marquee, think about having this as a wedding venue. Don't assume this is a cheaper option, however, and remember that it will mean a lot more for you to do. You'll need to hire your own caterers and bar staff, furniture, linen, glass and tableware, cutlery, and perhaps even portaloos. You'll also have to think about heating, lighting and power supply for the band or DJ. However, it can be a lovely option for couples who are tired of the same old venues but still want a big white wedding.

Celebrity Style

Ryanair CEO Michael O'Leary had four elegant marquees constructed in the grounds of his Georgian mansion for his wedding reception – one for the champagne reception, one for the meal, one for dancing, and another filled with comfy chairs for guests to take time out for a chat.

Keeping things Simple

If the idea of a big white wedding with maximum fuss fills you with horror, don't worry, it doesn't have to be that way. You have dozens of options for a much simpler, smaller – and cheaper – way of tying the knot.

Getting married abroad is an obvious solution; you get a wedding that's high on atmosphere and romance, and low on hassle. For more on this *see* Chapter 11.

But you don't have to go overseas to escape the fuss. All you need is a bit of creative thinking to come up with a wedding style that's simple and unique.

Think about having the meal in your favourite restaurant, and then going on somewhere for drinks and dancing. It may even be possible to book the whole restaurant (or a private room in the restaurant) and stay there for the night. It's certainly worth asking the manager, if the idea appeals to you.

Consider unusual venues such as an art gallery, a museum, a parish hall, the local golf or sailing club, a café, or a room above a pub. Some of these venues will make a sit-down meal impossible, but you could have a buffet, or limit the refreshments to drinks and finger foods.

Fidelma, Dublin

We chose a Georgian house café gallery in Dublin for our wedding reception. The flat next door was where we had first moved in together, and we had watched the owners of the house renovate it. At weekends we would see them moving antique furniture, and we got to know them by chatting on the steps of the house. We moved abroad a few years later, so having the wedding in a place we were so familiar with felt like a kind of homecoming.

Our families were a little dubious at first. They thought it would be easier to do what everyone else does, but we didn't want to have our reception in a hotel, as we tended to associate hotel venues with work.

So we hired the venue and had a champagne reception, followed by buffet meal, speeches and dancing. There were some seats, but not enough for everyone, so people perched in strange places and mixed and chatted with each other. It really encouraged our friends from different backgrounds to mingle. We were delighted with how it turned out on the day and feel our wedding will stand out in our guests' minds.

Have a small ceremony in a church or registry office, but instead of going straight to a reception, go off somewhere for the afternoon with your guests. You could have a day at the beach, a country walk or mountain hike, or, if you live in the city, head off to a matinee of a big musical.

Have a small, simple wedding ceremony, followed by a meal in a nice restaurant, with just those closest to you, and invite everyone else to a party when you come back from honeymoon. Many couples who get married abroad choose to do this when they come home, so there's no reason why you can't do the same.

Have an outdoor ceremony. You will have to be married in a registry office first, but there's no reason why your 'real' wedding can't be held outdoors – in your garden or a family member's garden, in a scenic location such as the Cliffs of Moher or the Hill of Tara (check with the local authorities first!) or in the garden of the hotel if you're having the reception there.

Celebrity Style

For her (gulp!) third wedding, Jennifer Lopez didn't tell anyone she was getting married – she just invited all her friends to a big party, and then surprised them by appearing in a white dress, with celebrant (and groom) to hand.

Claire, Wexford

Since I was a child I always said that my wedding and my mother's 'circus' would be on two different days. She is the best at organising parties, and whilst I love them, I did not fancy the fuss on my wedding day, especially since my husband is from Wales and comes from a small family and I have the typical large Irish family.

So, we got married on a Saturday with only thirty close family there and went back to a small country house where we had the run of things. On Sunday I had a party for 250 family and friends, and no one got left out.

CHAPTER THREE

How to Tie the Knot Without Breaking the Bank

U nless you happen to be marrying a member of Westlife – and you'd better move fast, girls, there aren't many of them left on the shelf – it's fairly unlikely that *Hello* are going to offer you a six-figure sum for your wedding photos. In fact, you will have to pay for the photos yourself – as well as for every other blessed thing you never knew you needed to tie the knot. You will be amazed at the number of wedding-related expenses that never even occurred to you before you started planning your own wedding. Too late you'll feel sympathy for the friend who would never go for pints after work because she was saving every penny to pay for buttonholes and vintage cars.

As early as possible in the planning process, work out a rough budget. This should include everything from rings to the honeymoon and be as comprehensive as possible, so that you can see from an early stage what the total is likely to be.

You will find an itemised **Budget Planner** on page 288, where you can keep track of your projected and actual costs as you confirm your various bookings. This will allow you to make cutbacks in one area, if you see another going way over budget.

Allow a bit extra for unexpected costs and build this into your budget to prevent worry later. There will always be things you haven't thought of, or that you only decide at a late stage that you simply must have.

Once you've recovered from the shock of seeing the size of your likely expenditure in black and white, take a cold look at your current finances and income. How many months are there until the Big Day? How much can you realistically save per month? If these two figures are completely incompatible, you may have to forego those swans on the lawn and the elaborate ice sculptures for every table.

Parents' Contribution

It may be that your parents or those of the groom would be happy – and possibly expect – to contribute to the cost of the wedding, but they often don't realise how early you need to know this to be able to start planning. Difficult though it may be, you should come right out and ask them so you know where you stand, unless, that is, you both have firm views on paying for the wedding yourselves.

Traditionally, the bride's parents were saddled with pretty much all of the expense. They were expected to pay for:

♥ Invitations, wedding booklets, place cards and any other stationery

♥ Bride's dress, veil, headdress, shoes and accessories

♥ Bridesmaids' dresses

♥ Wedding reception

♥ Cake

♥ Photographer

♥ Music for ceremony

♥ Flowers for the wedding venue

♥ Bride's trousseau

♥ Transport for bride and bridesmaids.

The groom was expected to pay for:

♥ Bride's engagement and wedding rings

♥ Bride and bridesmaids' bouquets

♥ Suit hire for the groom, best man and groomsmen

♥ Gifts for bridesmaids

♥ Church fees

♥ Honeymoon.

The bride's expenses were few. She, of course, was too busy crocheting doilies for her bottom drawer and learning to bake apple pie for her husband to bother her pretty little head with having a job.

However, times have moved on and any bride's parents reading this can breathe a sigh of relief. Nowadays, many couples pay for most if not all of the expenses themselves. While some parents wouldn't dream of allowing anyone else pay for their little girl's big day, others can't afford it, or simply believe it's not their responsibility, since their children are independent adults well capable of standing on their own two feet. Also, many brides and grooms feel they will be better able to retain control over the wedding plans if they finance it themselves.

Máirín, Co Wicklow

Announcing the engagement was extremely nerve-racking. Being such a Daddy's girl I knew he'd be pleased but heartbroken at the same time. Or maybe I was just flattering myself! However, I don't think I had prepared myself for his reaction. I now realise that his silence was covering pure panic as he wondered how much this day was going to cost him. After ten minutes or so he voiced the query that had obviously being rattling around his head: 'HOW MUCH?' I was very surprised that he would assume we expected him to pay and told him so. My parents were just getting to the stage where their income was their own. They had given us the best start in life possible and as a result I had a good job. I felt it would have been unfair of me to expect them to give anything other than their joy and blessing at our engagement. It would also have been a very dangerous precedent for him to set on the first wedding of five daughters. Now that wouldn't have been funny!

If you don't want any money from your parents you should also make this clear early on, as they may be worrying unnecessarily.

Nowadays, if the bride's parents *do* wish to contribute to the costs of the wedding, the most common practice is for them to pay for the reception, and possibly also the bride's outfit, with the bride and groom paying for the rest of the costs themselves. As for the bride's trousseau, the idea that a woman needs a whole new wardrobe to start off her married life has, sadly, died a death. Bring back the trousseau, say I – what a shame that this wonderful excuse to go shopping is a thing of the past.

Alternatively, the bride's parents might just give a specific sum to the couple who are then free to spend it on whichever area of the wedding they choose.

It's also very common now for the groom's parents to contribute towards the costs, or to pay for a specific item as a gift – perhaps the band or the photographer. And if there is a 'rehearsal dinner' – an American custom which is gathering popularity in Ireland – or a party the day after the wedding, it would be a nice gesture for the groom's parents to host or pay for this.

If you feel that accepting substantial contributions from parents may mean that you lose control over your plans, you might find it less stressful to tactfully refuse their offer of help. It might mean your wedding will be less lavish or that you have to save for a bit longer, but at least it will be your day.

Beat The Stress

Saving

Think of your wedding fund as a good way of getting into the saving habit! Try to save a minimum amount each month and put a little extra aside when you can. You will probably be lucky enough to receive cash as wedding presents, so if you have to do without certain things now, promise yourself a treat after the wedding.

Unless it's absolutely unavoidable, don't be tempted to borrow money to pay for your wedding. At the risk of sounding preachy, borrowed money is much easier to spend than your own hard-earned cash. It may allow you to splash out now, but do you really want to start married life in debt?

Your friends are all going to want to buy you a wedding present, so if you're finding it difficult to make ends meet, why not ask a few close friends to pay for something instead of a gift? There are only so many sets of John Rocha glasses a girl can use anyway. Perhaps your girlfriends would like to join together to pay for your flowers, or maybe your godparents would hire that harpist you feel you simply must have at the ceremony?

Whatever you do, don't fall into the trap of letting money worries take over your life. You don't have to stay in every night and live on beans on toast for the next twelve months. Think of fun things you can do with your future husband that don't cost too much (no, I wasn't talking about that, you naughty thing).

♥ Take long walks, which will allow you to unwind, tone up for your dress and spend some quality time together

♥ Take it in turns to show each other your favourite films on video – if he doesn't appreciate the wonders of *Dirty Dancing*, then he'd better learn to before he becomes your husband

♥ Rediscover your old hobbies – the ones that don't cost much but are a fun way of spending your free time.

Don't think you can't have a social life with your friends while saving – for one thing, you don't want to lose touch with your friends to the extent that you're wondering who to put on your guest list. Just think of ways you can socialise together without blowing your budget. Invite the girls around for a video night and a bottle of wine instead of going to the pub.

Where should we splash out, and where should we save?

This is very much a personal choice, and depends on which areas of the wedding are most important to you and your fiancé. Some brides spend a small fortune on their wedding dresses, arguing that it is the most important thing they will ever wear, while others are horrified at the idea of spending so much money on a dress that will be worn only once. Some consider the music one of the most important parts of the day, and want the top of the range string quartet, soprano, band and DJ.

One thing to remember is that apart from your wonderful memories, which are of course priceless, the only lasting material things you will take away from the day are your photos and your wedding rings, so most couples feel justified in spending a little more on those.

Remind yourself what the day is really all about: you and the man you love getting married in the company of people who care about you. Whether it costs €1,500 or €15,000 is not going to change that core fact. So don't lie awake at night worrying about the money aspect. A bride with bags under her eyes is not an attractive sight!

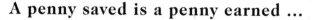

A penny saved is a penny earned ...

Use your imagination – and your contacts – to cut down on wedding bills.

Think about friends and relatives who you can ask for favours. Do you have a granny who could bake your wedding cake? An aunt who could sing at the ceremony? A friend with a fancy car who could drive you to the church? You will be pleasantly surprised by how enthusiastic people will be about helping to make your big day special.

€ If you live close enough to the church/registry office, don't bother getting a second car for the bridesmaids. Most car drivers will be happy to make two trips, leaving the bridesmaids there first, then coming back for you

€ Make your own stationery. Homemade invitations and booklets are more memorable as well as saving you money

€ Make your own favours, or don't bother with any. While they do give a nice extra touch to the reception, guests are unlikely to miss them if they're not there, and you would be surprised how many are left behind in hotels as people move from their own tables, get involved in the dancing, etc

€ Serve your wedding cake as dessert, if the venue allows

€ Do without a band, and have a DJ for the whole night. Better still, find a suitable friend who can borrow the equipment and be your DJ for the night

€ Hire your wedding dress and/or the bridesmaids' dresses, or buy them secondhand

€ Order your dresses over the internet – you can get great deals, from the US in particular. Try www.bridesave.com and www.gownsales.com

€ If you know someone who is a dab hand with a needle and thread, see if they'd be willing to help you out. Even if you have your heart set on a particular dress for yourself, how about getting them to make the bridesmaid dresses?

€ Invite only relatives and friends who you are close to

€ Don't invite your single friends 'plus guest' if they know other people at the wedding

€ Have sparkling wine instead of champagne for the toast

€ Think seriously about how many people you want to include in your bridal party – you may feel you simply must have all four of your sisters and your three closest friends as bridesmaids, but the cost of those dresses soon adds up.

You'll find more money-saving tips throughout the book – *see* in particular Chapters 7 and 8.

CHAPTER FOUR

The Bridal Party

W hatever about the venue, cake, flowers and dress – if you choose wisely, the people who make up your bridal party will give you the most wonderful memories of your wedding day and the weeks leading up to it. Unfortunately, a bad choice can also mean undue stress and hassle for the bride and groom, and even the souring of a beautiful friendship. This is why the task of choosing the right people for the job should be given at least as much thought and time as you put into organising other aspects of the day.

CHOOSING YOUR BRIDESMAIDS

How many?

Many weddings have just one bridesmaid, while it's also quite normal to have two, three or even four. Over that number is not very common in Ireland and might begin to look a tad OTT. While it was once the case that the number of bridesmaids was dictated by the size, formality and budget of the wedding itself, there is now a greater degree of flexibility on this issue.

Celebrity Style

At the wedding of John Magnier's daughter, Katie, there were no less than nine bridesmaids, all kitted out in Vera Wang dresses; at around €5,000 a pop, the bridesmaid dresses alone cost more than the average couple spend on their entire wedding.

However, if you are on a strict budget, bear in mind that bridesmaids are an expensive business, with dresses, shoes, gifts, hair and beauty treatments to be paid for, so be sensible and stick to a small number.

What should I look for in a bridesmaid?

A good bridesmaid will be enthusiastic about every aspect of your big day, will eagerly request updates on how your plans are progressing, will be an active organiser and participant in your hen party and any other pre-wedding events, and will be on hand to soothe and reassure you when wedding nerves set in. She will be flexible and recognise that even if she has her own unique style of dressing, this is your day and you make the choices.

A bad bridesmaid will show no interest in your wedding other than in her own dress, will try to ensure that said dress is entirely of her own choosing, will ignore your wishes and organise your idea of the hen party from hell, and will generally add to your stress and anxiety instead of easing it.

So do think carefully about which category your potential bridesmaid fits into before popping the question.

Who can I ask?

Essentially, you're not *obliged* to ask any particular person to be your bridesmaid. But, getting back to the real world here, if you have a sister, it is probably expected – both by her and by your mother – that she will be asked. If she has any of the traits of the good bridesmaid above, then she is the ideal person for the job, as she will not only be a wonderful support to you, but her involvement will help turn the wedding into a real family occasion.

However, if you haven't agreed on anything since you were four years old and are not close, then your best friend might be a more suitable choice. Yours may be a family that will accept this with good grace, but if you feel it will lead to bad feelings, then why not have both your best friend *and* your sister, but delegate all the responsible jobs to the best friend and get your mother to keep a tight rein on the sister if she becomes obstreperous.

Choosing among your friends can be difficult too, as you don't want anyone to feel hurt or disappointed. Be practical;

the friend to whom you entrust this important task should be someone you trust implicitly to tell you that you've got lipstick on your teeth, or that the dress you want to buy is a meringue of the fluffiest kind.

So what do you do if your best friend is a complete featherhead who is late for everything and never knows where anything is, but she is the only person who makes you laugh till it hurts? She may not be much help with selecting the ceremony readings, but you will have the best fun with her at your hen party and getting dolled up for the day. You know she would be hurt and you would feel guilty if you didn't ask her to be your bridesmaid – so it's far better that you do. Just balance things out with another sensible bridesmaid, and get the sensible one to have a word in her ear about doing her duty as a bridesmaid. In any case, no matter how scattered she is about most things, if she really cares about you she will make an extra special effort for the most important day of your life.

Celebrity Style

Madonna chose her chief bridesmaid very wisely – the role was filled by Stella McCartney, who also designed the wedding dress, details of which have never been made public.

Go with your gut instincts when choosing a bridesmaid – just give it some thought and discuss it with your fiancé, and possibly your mum, before asking her.

Do I have to ask my fiancé's sister?

It has become quite popular to ask your future sister-in-law to be one of your bridesmaids, but it's certainly not expected. Only ask her if you are very close and are friendly independently of your fiancé. Your bridesmaids are there to support you, and not the groom. If your fiancé is very close to his sister and wants to include her, perhaps she could be part of his party instead – maybe with the title Best Woman. Unorthodox, maybe, but weddings are not as conventional as they used to be. Or there are plenty of other ways to involve friends and family members who aren't part of the bridal party – more on this later.

WHAT DOES THE BRIDESMAID DO?

The chief bridesmaid – known as Maid of Honour in America, or Matron of Honour if she is married – plays the most important supporting role to the bride. She:

- ♥ Helps you choose your wedding dress, the bridesmaid dresses and flower girls' outfits, if any
- ♥ Organises the hen party after consulting with you
- ♥ Attends the wedding rehearsal
- ♥ Stays with you the night before the wedding if possible, so she can help calm your nerves and, more importantly, add to the sense of fun and anticipation
- ♥ Helps you get ready on the morning of the wedding
- ♥ Is waiting at the church/registry office when you arrive and checks that your veil, skirt, etc are perfect before you go in

♥ Keeps an eye on the flower girls and page boys, if there are any

♥ Holds your bouquet during the ceremony

♥ Stands with the bride and groom during the vows

♥ Signs the register as official witness to the marriage

♥ Accompanies the best man up the aisle

♥ Makes a speech at the reception, if you want her to

♥ Is available to run errands or deal with any problems that arise at the reception

♥ Helps you take off your veil and fix hair and make-up after the ceremony.

The chief bridesmaid should also help you put an emergency kit together (*see* Chapter 14). Some magazines and books will advise you that the chief bridesmaid should carry these around for you, but as my sister pointed out, she would have needed a rucksack to carry everything suggested, which would rather spoil the effect.

The other bridesmaids have similar roles, without the formalities undertaken by the chief bridesmaid. It's up to you how much you want to ask them to do – perhaps another bridesmaid would be better suited to organising the hen night, giving your chief bridesmaid one less thing to worry about.

If your bridesmaids have no experience of weddings, tell them what you want them to help with. Better still, type out a list for each of them and keep a copy. There's no point in you silently fuming that your bridesmaid isn't pulling her weight if she genuinely doesn't know what's expected of her.

Beat The Stress

CHOOSING THE BEST MAN

This is, of course, the groom's job, but there's no harm in putting a bit of thought into who would be right for the position. Your fiancé should check with you before asking him, just as you will have spoken to him about the choice of bridesmaids. Similar criteria to those for choosing a bridesmaid apply: someone who's trustworthy, responsible and cares about you, although hopefully he won't be called upon to tell your groom that he has lipstick on his teeth or is suffering from a bad case of VPL. Ultimately, it is the groom's choice, but try to nudge him in the direction of someone reliable!

WHAT DOES THE BEST MAN DO?

The best man has one of the most important and responsible jobs in any wedding day. He:

- ♥ Helps the groom to choose suits for himself and other male members of the bridal party
- ♥ Organises the stag party
- ♥ Attends the rehearsal
- ♥ Gets the groom to the church on time
- ♥ Collects the fees from the bride and groom to pay ceremony fees and other suppliers who need payment on the day, and distributes as appropriate
- ♥ Keeps an eye on the groomsmen and ushers
- ♥ Stands with the bride and groom during the vows
- ♥ Takes care of the rings and produces them at the appropriate moment

- Signs the register as official witness to the marriage
- Makes sure all the bridal party have transport to the reception
- Acts as the toastmaster – announcing the speeches, reading the cards and messages, and toasting the bride and groom in his speech
- Dances with the chief bridesmaid during the first bridal party dance
- Takes charge of any cards or gifts which guests bring to the reception
- Takes charge of the groom's suit after the wedding and returns it to the shop if hired, or has it dry cleaned
- Ensures everything runs smoothly at the reception and communicates with the hotel staff if necessary.

WHAT DOES THE GROOMSMAN DO?

The groomsman's duties are few. He:

- Attends the rehearsal
- Gets to the ceremony early
- Escorts guest to their seats and hands out the wedding booklets, unless there are ushers on hand to do this
- Stands with the bride and groom during the vows
- Supports the best man in any way necessary
- You could also give the groomsman a specific task to take the pressure off the best man, such as looking after the band or DJ.

Do we have to have the same number of bridesmaids and groomsmen?

There is a nice symmetry in having the same number of attendants lined up beside the bride and groom, but it is certainly not essential. The only times it will be noticed is in walking back up the aisle after the ceremony, posing for photographs, and during the first dance with the bridal party. Decide how much it bothers you that these parts of the day are perfectly matched. You'll probably find it is more important that each of you has the people closest to you involved, rather than asking someone extra, or leaving someone out, just to make numbers match.

If you end up with an extra bridesmaid, then let the lucky best man walk up the aisle with a woman on each arm. For the bridal party dance, an extra groomsman can dance with his own partner or with a member of the bride or groom's family.

We were at a friend's wedding where there was one bridesmaid, a best man and a groomsman. The bride wanted to have her sister but didn't want to choose among her friends for a second bridesmaid, whereas the groom wanted his two best friends involved. As the groom's mother was a widow, the groomsman accompanied her on the walk up the aisle, and danced with her for the bridal party dance – it was a really lovely touch.

BRIDAL PARTY COSTS

Do we have to pay for everything?

In Ireland, it's usual for the bride and groom to pay for the bridesmaid's dress and accessories, her hair and make-up, if done professionally, and a thank-you gift. Shoes are debatable – if you want your bridesmaid to wear a specific pair to match the dress, you should pay for them. If a more neutral pair would go with the dress, such as strappy black sandals, which she would definitely wear again, then it's fine to ask her to buy them herself – of course this isn't possible in all cases.

Bridesmaids should cover their own travel and accommodation expenses. After all, they would still be travelling to the wedding as your friend even if they weren't part of the bridal party.

Often bridesmaids will offer to pay for some things themselves, such as hair and make-up, or any alterations required to their dresses. Discuss this with them if they offer, and do whatever you all feel comfortable with.

It's also usual for the bride and groom to cover the costs of suit hire for the male members of the bridal party if they are dressing in formal wear.

ROLES FOR CHILDREN

You may have nieces and nephews, children of close friends, or even your own little darlings who you want to include in your wedding. Girls aged between three and eight can be flower girls, and will certainly steal the show. Boys of this age can be page boys or ring bearers (though they tend to grow out of being willing to dress up and look cute a lot earlier than girls).

Older girls, aged ten to fifteen, could be junior bridesmaids. It's hard to find a formal role for boys of this age, but they could do a reading, or hand out wedding booklets.

Try to pick children who you know will be well behaved and

won't chase each other around the altar or try to add their own sound effects to the music. Ensure that either the chief bridesmaid or their parents will be on hand to keep them in line if necessary.

INVOLVING OTHER PEOPLE IN YOUR WEDDING

You won't be able to include everyone who's important to you in the bridal party, but there are plenty of other things you can ask them to do, which will make them feel special, and you feel pleased that they're a big part of your day. Here are some possibilities:

If it is a church ceremony – bringing up the gifts, acting as readers or leading the prayers of the faithful. *See* Chapter 6 for more on this.

Making or icing the wedding cake, singing at the ceremony, flower arranging, dressmaking, providing or driving one of the wedding cars, lending you accessories or jewellery, making favours. It's nice to think that while they're saving you work and money, they're also pleased to be involved.

Acting as ushers. Ushers are usually male, though they don't have to be. They show guests to their seats (bride to the left, groom to the right) and distribute wedding booklets, and afterwards hand out confetti, bubbles etc. As a rough guideline, you should have one usher for every fifty guests. It makes sense to have one usher from the groom's side and one from the bride's, so that between them they'll know most of the guests.

Signing the register: it's usually the chief bridesmaid and the best man who sign the register, but maybe you'd like to ask someone else instead. Your father will already have had a role in giving you away, but the groom's father won't, so it might be a nice thought to have the two dads sign the register, or the two mums for that matter.

GETTING THE GROOM INVOLVED

Now, this may not be your experience, but people I have spoken to confirm that with most weddings there are two people deeply interested in every little detail – the bride and her mother. Yes, it's the groom's day as well, but most grooms have to be reminded of that time and again. He'll probably tell you you're doing such a good job you obviously don't need his help, and that he'd only mess it up anyway!

Traditionally, the groom is supposed to organise the honeymoon, so if he's not getting involved in the wedding plans, at least get him to do that. Alas, my husband managed to leave that in my hands too. I even had to drag him into the suit hire shop to get him to choose his own suit. You can look at this behaviour in one of two ways: find it extremely irritating and let it get you into a tizzy, or look on the bright side and be happy that you have a free hand in choosing your paradise destination or that shade of deep navy waistcoat that he would never have dreamed of picking.

The only thing my beloved was really interested in was the music for the evening reception – he made so many lists of songs he wanted played that the wedding would have had to last an entire week if we were to have them all. So I gave him the job of finding a band. However, I still wanted to be involved (it's hard to let go of the Bridezilla mantle) and went along to check out different bands with him, but he was in charge of calling them to find out when they were playing, taking notes, booking the band we selected, and making all the follow-up calls. Meanwhile, I handled the five hundred and seventy-three other tasks, or so it seemed.

Men, it would appear, are not interested in weddings. Sure, they want to stand up and declare their love for you in front of their families and friends, and have a huge party afterwards to celebrate, but they really don't care too much about how it all comes together.

Remember that marriage is all about compromise, so start as you mean to go on with regard to division of labour. It's really not fair that one party has to do all the work. The groom should sort out his own invitation list in good time, including guests his parents want to invite. And that doesn't mean writing the names on the back of the sports section; it means getting all the addresses and phone numbers. As I found with the music, it's best to ask the groom to take care of an area that he's interested in. For some men, it might be the wedding cars, the videographer or selecting the wine.

For an insight into what men really think about weddings *see* Chapter 13.

Make plenty of time for the two of you as a couple. If things are getting on top of you, plan a weekend away, or if funds are tight make it a relaxing weekend at home without seeing anyone else, and where the wedding is completely banned as a topic of conversation.

Beat The Stress

The Exceptional Groom

If your husband-to-be sound nothing like those I've mentioned above and does his fair share of all the wedding planning, all I can say is lucky you, and please try not to gloat over those brides less fortunate than yourself.

WHAT DO THE PARENTS DO?

Mother of the Bride

Traditionally, the mother of the bride would do much of the organising, from arranging the engagement party to picking out the invitations and planning the reception. Nowadays most couples like to take charge of these things themselves, but there are still many ways to get your mother involved. Ask her advice at every stage, bring her dress shopping, bring her to meetings with the florist, photographer and cakemaker, and get her to draw up a list of those she and your father would like to invite.

Your mother will also be invaluable after the wedding for things like taking your dress to the dry cleaners and looking after any wedding presents you haven't brought to your own home as yet.

Mother of the Groom

The only task which is traditionally the groom's mother's is to host a meal or party of some kind for the bride and her family, either shortly after the engagement, or around the time of the wedding – often after the rehearsal.

However, it's nice to involve her in the preparations too, as long as she's willing – maybe ask her opinion on the flowers or the bridesmaid dresses. Mothers of grooms can feel a bit left out of the plans. Be particularly sensitive if you are marrying her 'one and only', as she will not get another such opportunity. At the very least, do make sure that your future mother-in-law is kept up to date on what's happening; let her know whether most of the women attending the wedding will be wearing hats, and – very important – the colour and style of your mother's outfit. Both mothers in your life will be unlikely to forgive you if they arrive at the church in identical attire.

Obviously, the involvement of either mother will be much more limited if both bride and groom live – and are marrying – away from their home areas. You will have to work even harder to keep the lines of communication and information open so that both still feel included.

Father of the Bride

The father of the bride plays one of the most important roles, both formally and informally. He walks the bride down the aisle (though many brides get both parents to do this nowadays) and makes a speech after the meal, but he also generally acts as taxi driver to out-of-town guests or as delivery man for flowers, decorations and favours, helps to draw up the guest list, and perhaps helps you out with the map and directions for guests. At the reception he should also dance with his own wife, your new mother-in-law and, of course, you.

Father of the Groom

The father of the groom has very little in the way of a formal role, but again you can involve him as much as you want. He can help the groom's mother with drawing up the guest list and any other tasks you've delegated to their family.

Helpful Parental Contacts

If your parents or the groom's parents have contacts – either through their own businesses or otherwise – with suppliers (florists, printers, wine merchants, the car hire industry, etc), they will probably be more than happy to organise discounts or special rates for you. This could make a substantial dent in your wedding expenses and be seen as their contribution to costs.

How much should parents get involved?

I really don't know what I would have done without my mother to help with the wedding plans. She modestly claims that she did very little, but in fact she did so many of the things that I couldn't do because I was living a four-hour drive away from where we were getting married: collecting and dropping things off, organising alterations on bridesmaid dresses, setting up appointments, and generally making sure that things ran smoothly. And she managed to do all this without interfering in any way with the actual plans.

I realise that I'm very lucky and that there are brides-to-be out there who are tearing their hair out because their mothers are a) attempting to take over the wedding, or b) showing no interest at all in their plans.

If your mother is the interfering kind, listen calmly to any advice or suggestions. If it's not what you want to do, thank her politely for her concern but say that you and your fiancé have discussed it and have agreed what you're going to do. Never underestimate the importance of presenting a united front. This also works on fathers, mothers-in-law, fathers-in-law and any other people who feel that they could do it so much better than you can.

If your mother is being very detached about the wedding, try to talk to her about it – there could well be a reason behind what appears to you to be a strange attitude. Maybe she's afraid of being seen as the interfering type and as a result she's gone to the other extreme. Maybe she is sad about the whole idea of you being all grown up and part of another family; blocking out the wedding plans is her way of dealing with that. Try to reassure her that you want her help, you value her opinion, and that she will always be an important part of your life. Bring her dress shopping with you, take time to pick out her outfit with her, and consider delegating a task to her, such as sorting out the flowers.

Bach Rescue Remedy is a bride's best friend. Made from flowers and distilled in brandy, it's designed to keep you calm in times of stress.

With friends like these, who needs enemies?

Weddings bring out the best in many people. Unfortunately, they also bring out the worst in others. Family rows that you thought were long forgotten will resurface and you'll be told you can't possibly invite your Aunt Mary because she refused to lend your mother maternity clothes when she was expecting you!

Friends can be just as bad. It's a cliché but it's true – you definitely find out who your real friends are at times like this. Some won't be able to do enough for you: going shopping with you in their lunchbreaks, listening to you talk for hours on end about which shade of pink would be best, and ringing you regularly with offers of help. Others will show a complete lack of interest that can be very hurtful. Worst of all are the so-called friends who make nasty comments about your choice of venue, fabric or even husband.

Try not to let such comments hurt you. You're happy. You're doing things the way you want, so ask yourself whether this person's opinion really matters.

And remember the other cliché – you can please some of the people some of the time, but you can't please all of the people all of the time. With wedding plans it's impossible to keep everyone happy. You can only do your best to ensure they'll all enjoy the day, but remember that it's the two of you that really matter.

CHAPTER FIVE

Legal and Religious Requirements

MAKE IT LEGAL

N ow for the boring, but essential part: sorting out the legal requirements for getting married. First, a word of caution: no book can cover every circumstance and, as will become clear when you read on, the least complicated scenario is where both parties are of the same religious faith or none, and have not been married before. Even then, the requirements can appear quite involved. So, in *all* cases, and whether the marriage is to be by civil or religious ceremony, the best and most important advice to a couple planning their wedding is to get in touch with the officiant/celebrant as early as possible. They will have all the necessary information regarding what you need to do. The last thing you want is for your plans to be completely overturned because you have left it too late to get a licence, permission, or other required documentation.

Marriage law in Ireland – Changes

You may have heard that reform of the marriage law in Ireland is under way and are wondering how this will affect your plans?

Yes, changes are coming, (*see* box across) and one way in which they will impact on your plans will be to make a much wider range of venues available for civil marriages, which will no longer be confined to registry offices. However, there is no definite date for when the new rules will be in place. At the time of going to print, the best information available was that it would be late 2005 or early 2006, and the advice from the General Register Office, who are in charge of making the changes, is that you should not make plans on the assumption that the new rules will be in place for the time of your civil wedding, but proceed on the basis that your civil wedding must be in a registry office. They say that they 'recognise the fact that people make arrangements for their marriages well in advance of the event' so intend to give as much notice as possible of the new rules, and that they will be mounting a 'comprehensive public information campaign at the appropriate time.' In the meantime, you can check their website, www.groireland.ie for the latest updates on the state of play.

REFORM OF THE MARRIAGE LAW

Under the Civil Registration Act 2004, changes will to be made to the rules relating to **who can solemnise a marriage, where marriages can take place, how marriages are registered** and other matters such as the **requirements for a period of residency** in the district where the marriage will take place.

Civil marriage ceremonies will no longer be confined to registry offices. With the agreement of the person conducting the wedding (called 'the registered solemniser' in the Act), you will be able to get married in a much wider variety of places, such as hotels, parks, castles etc, as long as the venue is suitable, is open to the public, conforms with fire and safety regulations and any necesssary permission from owners etc is forthcoming. 'Suitable' means somewhere that reflects the solemnity of the occasion – so bouncy castles, bungee jumps and parachuting ceremonies will still be out.

The legal requirements set out in this chapter are those currently in force and do not take into account any changes that may be made under the new legislation.

THE BASICS

For a marriage to be legally valid in Ireland, the parties must have the capacity to marry each other, freely consent to the marriage, and observe the necessary formalities.

The 'capacity to marry each other' means that you and your groom-to-be must be 18 years of age or older; be either single, widowed or divorced in Ireland, or have a State annulment or a valid foreign divorce; be of the opposite sex; and not be related by blood or marriage to a degree that prohibits a marriage between you.

Under 18?

It used to be that persons over the age of 16 could marry if they had their parents' consent, but this is no longer the case. Currently, the only way in which someone under 18 can be legally married in Ireland is if they get a Court Exemption Order – parental consent is not an issue, whatever the age of the parties.

NOTIFICATION TO THE STATE

You must give the State three months' notice of your intention to marry, by informing – in writing – the registrar of the district in which you plan to be married. This rule applies to all couples, whether they intend to be married in a religious ceremony or in a registry office. (An additional notification is required for registry office marriages, explained under the heading *Getting Married by Civil Ceremony*)

There are two registrars for each district: for Catholic

ceremonies, the Registrar of Births, Deaths and (Roman Catholic) Marriages; for registry office weddings and other religious ceremonies recognised by the State, the Registrar of Civil Marriages. You must send the notification to the appropriate registrar for the form of wedding you are planning.

The General Register Office will be able to give you the name of the Registrar for your area. They can be contacted at:

The General Register Office
Government Offices
Convent Road
Roscommon
Tel 0906632900
Fax 0906632999

The simplest way to send notification of intent to marry is to complete a pre-printed form (known as the green form), which you can have sent out to you by calling the Registrar of Births, Marriages and Deaths in the district in which you intend to marry, or print it off from www.oasis.gov.ie. You must both sign this form, or each of you can complete a separate form.

Alternatively, you can write, jointly or separately, to the Registrar, including your names and addresses, dates of birth, the church or other place where the wedding will take place, the name of the person who will perform the ceremony, and the date of the wedding. If either of you has been married before, you need to inform them of this also.

The Registrar will send you both a dated acknowledgement of your notification. Keep this document, as you'll need to give it to the celebrant who is conducting your wedding ceremony.

Remember that the Registrar must have received your

notification at least three months before your wedding date (unless there are special circumstances, as outlined below). However, you can send it as early as you like, so it makes sense to get it out of the way as soon as you've confirmed the date and place of the marriage and the name of the celebrant.

Exemptions from the three-month notice rule

In some special circumstances, such as where one of the parties is seriously ill, you may be able to get a Court Exemption Order to allow the marriage to go ahead without the three months' notification. You will need to get in touch with the Circuit Family Court or the High Court in your area to apply for this. It is an informal procedure, so you don't need to hire a solicitor. The Court requires you to show that there are good reasons for the application and that the order is in the best interests of both of you.

CAN I BE LEGALLY MARRIED WHEREVER I LIKE?

The simple answer is no. As the law currently stands, a legally valid marriage in Ireland has to be either a civil ceremony in a registry office or a religious ceremony that is also recognised by civil law as a civil contract.

What this means for a civil ceremony is that you cannot simply pick a historic building, scenic location or particular hotel that takes your fancy and be legally married there as is possible in other countries. You may be able to have a ceremony or blessing in some such location if you can find someone willing to act as celebrant, but this won't be legally binding and you will have to get married in a registry office also. Even when the law changes to broaden the range of venues available (*See* box page 76) your choice will still be restricted to locations that are approved as 'suitable'.

Religious denominations whose marriage ceremonies are recognised by civil law as legally valid include:

Roman Catholic
Church of Ireland
Methodist
Presbyterian
Baptist
Society of Friends
Jewish Communities

(Some other churches also come under the umbrella of those named above, for example, the Unitarian Church is encompassed by the Presbyterian Church.)

If you are a member of a faith whose marriage ceremonies are not recognised for legal purposes, you can still have a religious ceremony in your own church, but you must also have a civil ceremony in order to be legally married.

GETTING MARRIED BY CIVIL CEREMONY

A marriage by civil ceremony must take place in the office of a Registrar of Civil Marriages (registry office). There is one of these offices in each county.

The first thing you need to do is to 'serve notice' of your

intention to marry. This is not the same as the three-month notification which all couples intending to marry must give the State. (*See* page 77) You have to make an appointment to see the Registrar and serve notice in person. If you both live in different districts, you must serve notice on the Registrar of both districts.

You can get married either by Registrar's Licence or Registrar's Certificate. The only essential difference between the two options is the residency requirements.

Registrar's Licence

In order to get married by Registrar's Licence, at least *one* of you must have lived in the district in which the marriage is to take place for *at least fifteen days* before serving notice. The other person must have lived there for *at least seven days*. If you both live in different districts then both of you must have had a residence of *at least fifteen days* in the district in which the marriage is to take place, before service of notice. The marriage may not take place until the eighth day at the earliest after the entry of notice by the Registrar.

Registrar's Certificate

In order to get married by Registrar's Certificate, you must *both* have lived in the district in which the marriage is to take place for *at least seven days* before serving notice. This applies whether you live in the same district or not. The marriage may not take place until the twenty-second day at earliest after you have served notice.

Once you have fulfilled these obligations, there is no expiry date on your entitlement to get married in that district. Therefore, this is something you can do as early as you like in your preparations.

When you go to the Registrar's Office to serve notice of marriage, you may be asked to show:

- Your birth certificate
- Your passport or driving licence
- Proof of residency – if you live in the area, a bill or a bank statement will do. If you are coming from abroad, you should produce your plane ticket showing when you arrived in Ireland, and a receipt or note on headed paper from where you are staying.
- If you are widowed or divorced, the death certificate of your spouse or the divorce decree.

GETTING MARRIED BY RELIGIOUS CEREMONY

Each religion has its own requirements and you should contact your local clergy as soon as possible for advice on how to proceed.

CATHOLIC CHURCH

One of the first things you will have to do is to contact the priest of the church you have chosen to see if it is available for the day you want, and book it accordingly. (As mentioned earlier in this book, if this church is outside your own parish, then you may have to notify the priest of your parish as well). One thing which is not always made clear to couples is that you also need to book the priest, particularly if there is more than one attached to the parish. If either of you has a relative or friend who is a priest and who you want to celebrate the marriage, you should discuss this with the parish priest at an early date.

If you are booking your wedding well in advance, the priest will probably tell you to contact him again about four to six months before the wedding day to discuss the church requirements for marriage, the ceremony, and any other questions you may have.

The pre-marriage course

Most, though not all, parishes require you to attend a pre-marriage course in preparation for your wedding. Couples generally dread these, but they're really not as bad as they sound, and can even be quite enjoyable (yes, really). Pre-marriage courses are generally booked up three or four months in advance – sometimes more – so make sure you book one in plenty of time.

There are several different types of pre-marriage course. Some take place in the evening over several weeks. Others are on over a weekend, or on a Friday evening and all day Saturday. Most are based on the 'five Cs' – church, commitment, communication, conflict and children, and are run by lay married people and a priest. You won't be expected to speak about anything personal in front of the group, just with your partner. Other courses involve the couple meeting privately with the course facilitator.

Try to go into the course with an open mind and remember that with all the time you're spending planning your wedding, which is just one day, this is the only part that is preparing you for your marriage, which will last a lifetime.

At the end of the course you will be given a certificate to say that you completed the course, and this is one of the documents you'll be asked to produce at the pre-nuptial enquiry.

Some priests don't insist that you attend a pre-marriage

course, and others will make exceptions in some circumstances, for example if you already have a child together.

Baptism and Confirmation Certificates

You will need to provide the priest with your baptism and confirmation certificates, and these must carry a date of issue that is not less than six months before the date of your marriage.

In case you're wondering why, the thinking behind this is that your parish of baptism keeps a record of all the important events in your life as a Catholic – even if you moved away as a child. The church where you made your First Holy Communion and your Confirmation will have sent this information to the parish where you were baptised. Equally, they will be informed when you get married – so obtaining the certificates no more than six months before your wedding helps reassure the priest that you haven't been married before.

You can ring or write to the parish(es) where you were baptised and confirmed and ask them to post you out the certificates. If you or your parents can't remember the exact dates, don't worry – just give as much information as you can and they will be able to track down your records.

Letters of freedom

Most parishes require you to get a letter of freedom (a statement that you have not been married before) from the parish priest of the parish where you live, *and* for any parish where you have lived as an adult for more than six months. If you lived away from home as a student but regularly returned home for weekends and holidays, the priest will usually be willing to regard your home parish as your place of residence for this period, and won't require an additional letter of freedom. If you've lived in a large number of different parishes and getting letters of freedom from them all is impractical, the priest may be willing to accept an affidavit, or sworn statement, from you that you haven't been married before. Contact a solicitor to arrange this.

The pre-nuptial enquiry form

You need to make an appointment to see the priest in the parish where you are living, even if that's not where you are getting married, and he will fill in a pre-nuptial enquiry form for you. You need to supply him with your baptism and confirmation certificates, letters of freedom, pre-marriage course completion certificate (if required), and the acknowledgement from the Registrar that you have given the required State notification of your intention to marry.

The priest will ask for all relevant details, including your addresses, dates of birth, occupations, parents' names and addresses, and the names and addresses of the best man and chief bridesmaid, if you intend them to be the witnesses to the marriage. Most priests won't bat an eyelid if your addresses indicate that you are living together, but if you're really worried about this, one of you could give your parents' address – though it has to be said that honesty is the best policy! Also, this information is what will appear on your civil marriage certificate, so it's important to make sure all the details are correct – if you think he's written something down incorrectly, say so now!

You will then be asked a number of questions about your

faith, your intention to continue to practice your faith as a married couple, and to bring your children up as Catholics. There's no need to be worried about this – the questions aren't too probing, and the priest is mainly concerned to establish that you understand the serious nature of entering into a Catholic marriage.

If you're getting married in a different parish, the priest will send on all the documentation to the priest in that parish.

What if one of us is not a Catholic?

If one of you is not a Catholic, you can still get married in a Catholic Church, but in most cases you will need a dispensation from the bishop. This can be arranged by your priest and is usually just a formality, but make sure you do it in plenty of time.

The Catholic partner is asked to promise to try to bring any children of the marriage up as Catholics, but the non-Catholic partner does not have to make this promise.

If the non-Catholic partner is a member of another Christian church, his/her minister can take part in the wedding ceremony, with the agreement of the priest.

The ceremony can be just the same as any other Catholic wedding, although some couples choose to have a wedding service without Mass, as any guests who are not Catholics would be unable to receive Communion.

If you do decide to have a wedding Mass, you can request the permission of the bishop for the non-Catholic partner to receive communion, if they are a member of another Christian church.

What if one of us has been married before?

If you would like to have a church wedding but have been married before and are divorced, then it is extremely unlikely that you will be able to have a Catholic wedding. As a general rule, the Catholic Church does not allow divorced persons to be married in church. However, it may be that your original marriage was not recognised as valid by the Catholic Church, or there are other circumstances relating to your situation that may make a difference. Each case is examined on its merits by specialists in canon law, and you should contact the Chancery Office, The Archbishop's House, Drumcondra, Dublin 9, tel 01-8373732 or 01-8379253. Other dioceses also have chancery offices, so check with your local clergy.

The only sure way, as a Catholic, that you will be able to remarry in a Catholic church is if you have been granted a church annulment. Annulments are granted for a variety of reasons, including:

- The person did not marry of their own free will
- There was a lack of commitment to the permanence of the marriage
- Vital information was withheld from one partner.

As anyone who has sought an annulment will tell you, it can be a very long and messy business; you will not be given any guarantee of how long it will take or if the annulment will even be granted. If you have already started down the road to an annulment and have your heart set on a full Catholic wedding, then I'm afraid you will have to wait and hope.

You may, however, be given permission to have a church blessing, which will be a ceremony very similar to a normal wedding, but will not be a legal marriage contract, therefore you will have to get married in a registry office as well.

If you do secure the church annulment, you will also need to give the priest evidence of a civil annulment or divorce.

CHURCH OF IRELAND

You may be legally married in the Church of Ireland in one of the following ways:

- By ordinary ecclesiastical licence – one of you must serve notice on the Licenser of Marriages from the district in which the marriage will take place. One or both of you must live in the district for a specified period, and one or both of you must be members of the Church of Ireland
- By special licence, granted by the Church of Ireland Bishops – this is issued where an ordinary licence is not appropriate because of non-residency reasons, or in other exceptional circumstances
- After publication of the banns – this requires that you are both members of the Church of Ireland and one of you is living in the parish where the marriage is to take place
- On production of a certificate from a Registrar of Civil Marriages – you must serve notice on the Registrar of Civil Marriages and follow the same steps as you would for a civil ceremony. You then show the certificate to your minister.

Note: These licensing arrangements will become part of the civil procedure when the changes to the marriage law under the Civil Registration Act 2004 are implemented.

What if one of us was married before?

There are limited possibilities for remarriage of divorced persons in the Church of Ireland. Each case is examined on its merits and you should contact your local rector who will advise on whether it may be possible in your situation.

Anita, Dublin

We decided on our venue of Kilkea Castle after falling in love with its location and ambience. We were devastated to discover that we could not officially marry in church in Ireland because Tony was a divorcé and we had mixed religious backgrounds. We were still determined not to lose our special day, so the decision was made to have a simple and very intimate registry office celebration in Chester, with just our best man, our niece and our son attending. It was in itself an emotional experience that set the tone for the ceremony in Ireland to follow.

The blessing, which took place in the beautiful church at Kilkea, will always be remembered as our real wedding day, surrounded by all our family and friends and our handsome son Carl walking me down the aisle to my gorgeous husband. It was a beautiful day and all our disappointment and upset were truly forgotten.

So now we have three anniversaries in June. The 7th, which is the civil marriage, the 13th, which celebrates the day we met, and the 14th, which we regard as our wedding proper.

PRESBYTERIAN CHURCH

You may be legally married in the Presbyterian Church in one of the following ways:

- By ordinary ecclesiastical licence – one of you must serve notice on the Licenser of Marriages from the district in which the marriage will take place. One or both of you must live in the district for a specified period, and one or both of you must be members of the Presbyterian Church
- By special licence, granted by the Moderators of the Presbyterian Church
- After publication of the banns – this requires that you are both members of the Presbyterian Church.

JEWISH

You may be legally married under the Jewish faith in one of the following ways:

- On production of a certificate from a Registrar of Civil Marriages – you must serve notice on the Registrar of Civil Marriages and follow the same steps as you would for a civil ceremony. You must then show the certificate to your Rabbi
- By special licence, granted by the Chief Rabbi.

SOCIETY OF FRIENDS/QUAKERS

You may be legally married under the Quaker faith in one of the following ways:

- On production of a certificate from a Registrar of Civil Marriages – you must serve notice on the Registrar of Civil Marriages and follow the same steps as you would for a civil ceremony. You must then show the certificate to your minister
- By special licence, granted by the Clerk to the yearly meeting.

THE UNITARIAN CHURCH
Can people who have been previously married get married there?

You have probably read in the papers that people have been able to have second marriages celebrated in the Unitarian church on St Stephen's Green in Dublin. The minister and named lay preachers of the Unitarian Church are allowed to perform legal marriages, and they *will* marry previously married people. (Obviously, the couple will have to be legally entitled to re-marry in the first place.) One of the parties must make a declaration to the registrar of marriages that he/she is a Unitarian or Presbyterian. The Church is a non-creedal church. There are no tests of belief and no ceremony of admittance. Membership is open to those who wish to be regarded as members. *See* their website at www.unitarianchurchdublin.org.

There is also a Unitarian church on Prince's Street in Cork, but it does not have a resident licensed marriage officiant.

For any further details you should contact the Unitarian Church, 112 Stephens Green West, Dublin 2. Tel: 01 4780638.

CREATE YOUR OWN WEDDING CEREMONY

There is no reason why you cannot have a ceremony that is non-religious; for example, you may wish to have a Humanist wedding ceremony. (For information, contact The Humanist Association, tel. 01-2869870.) However, it is important to remember that if you choose this option you will not be *legally* married, so you will also have to have a civil ceremony in a registry office.

NORTHERN IRELAND

The legal requirements relating to marriage in Northern Ireland are broadly similar, but if you have any queries, check out www.groni.gov.uk or contact The Marriage Section, General Register Office, Oxford House, 49-55 Chichester Street, Belfast BT1 4HL. Tel: (028) 9025 2036/37

GETTING MARRIED ABROAD

For legal requirements for weddings abroad, *see* Chapter 11.

CHAPTER SIX

'I Do':
The Ceremony

Before you get too caught up in things like menus, dresses and sparkly tiaras, put some thought into what kind of wedding ceremony you want. This, after all, is the part of the day where you get to stand up in front of all those you care about and promise to spend the rest of your lives together. By now you've made the major decisions about what form of ceremony you're having, where it will take place, and who will perform it for you. And whether you've opted for a church wedding or a civil ceremony, there are plenty of ways to put your personal stamp on proceedings. Readings, music, the form of vows you choose, how you decorate the venue, and who you involve, all help to make the ceremony uniquely yours.

For religious weddings, it is important that you meet with the celebrant at an early stage to find out how much input you can have. Church weddings have to follow a certain format, and there will be limitations on your choice of readings, music and so on; find out what you can and can't do before you set your heart on something. Each religion has its own set of rules, so it's best to talk to your own celebrant.

Civil ceremonies are more flexible, but there are still certain procedures that have to be followed, so again it would be wise to meet with the celebrant before planning too much. In particular, you need to get the wording that you are *required* to include in your vows, so you can then set about deciding on the personalised bits of the ceremony. Also, bear in mind that there will be time constrictions on the length of the ceremony, so be realistic about how much extra you can include, as you don't want the proceedings to have to go at breakneck speed just to fit everything in.

As I mentioned in previous chapters, many couples who opt for a civil wedding decide to have another ceremony as well as the registry office one. For this second ceremony, you can let your imagination run wild – as it's not a legal occasion, you can organise it any way you want. If you want to hold it in the garden at midnight by the light of a full moon, or have it performed entirely in mime, that's completely up to you (and it would certainly ensure your wedding would be one to remember).

YOUR CEREMONY, STEP BY STEP

Setting the scene

Flowers are the most effective way to decorate the venue. For church weddings, discuss with the celebrant what flower arrangements you can have in the church, and when you or your florist can put them in place. These can be as simple as one or two arrangements on the altar, or as elaborate as half a dozen scattered around the church, at pew ends, and a bridal arch or bay trees on your way in. It all depends on what's appropriate for (and allowed by) the particular church and how much you want to spend. You could also consider placing candles around the church, as they can create a wonderful atmosphere, especially for evening or winter weddings.

You may be lucky with the time of year you're getting married – the altar society might have the church decorated for Christmas, Easter, the Harvest Festival etc. Check with the celebrant – there's no point in going to too much trouble if someone else will do it for you! However, bear in mind that your wedding may be coinciding with First Communions or Confirmations, which can mean that your church is decorated with the handprints of several classes of eight or twelve-year-olds, plus their photos. If you are OK with that, fine, but otherwise it might be worth checking with the celebrant.

In a registry office, you don't normally need to bring flowers, as they usually have some in place already, but check with the celebrant. If the flowers they normally use are artificial, you may want to replace them for your day.

See Chapter 7 for advice on choosing your flowers.

Seating in the church

The bride's family and friends sit on the left hand side of the aisle and the groom's on the right, according to tradition. In the old days, marriage was often used to bring two warring tribes together, so it was considered safer to keep the families apart, in order to prevent any fighting in the church! Unless you feel you might have this problem, you don't have to stick to this formula, especially if one group is much larger than the other and it would make the seating look very unbalanced. There are usually chairs in front of the first row of pews for the bridesmaids, best man and groomsmen, and, of course, in the centre for the bride and groom. Parents sit in the first row, with close family beside or behind them.

The ushers should show guests to their seats and hand out wedding booklets. (*See* Chapter 4 on the role of the usher).

Think about having music playing as the guests arrive, and the type of music it should be, as this helps create the atmosphere.

In the old days, the groom used to kidnap his bride, and hold her on his left arm so that his sword arm was free to fight off any other suitors. This is why the groom normally stands to the right of the bride during the wedding ceremony.

A Little Bit of History

Should the bride be late?

Over time, a tradition has been established that the bride is roughly ten minutes late for the ceremony and many brides wouldn't dream of breaking with this custom. However, you may feel that there is no reason in the world to be late and hold people up, and this is certainly a view that would be welcomed by officiating clergy or registrars. In fact, one priest has been known to walk out in protest at waiting over half an hour and had to be persuaded to come back by the father of the bride.

Whichever view you hold, it is reasonable to suggest that being any more than fifteen minutes late is a bit rude to your guests – not to mention the poor groom quaking in his new shoes at the altar – and it may cause ongoing delays to the rest of the day. It's best to plan to be on time; you never know what delays could strike en route to the ceremony, and you can always circle the block if you're too early. Everyone loves a bride, so you will have nothing but smiles and waves as you make your tour! Remember also that you will be having photographs taken when you arrive, which will take a few more minutes.

If yours is the only wedding at the venue, you will have more leeway in terms of time, but if there is another wedding after yours then it's really not fair to hold it up and it will cause complete confusion after your ceremony, as your guests get caught up with the other party.

Do make sure that your ushers have shepherded the guests to their seats before you arrive, as people have become accustomed to the bride being late and are inclined to hang around outside the church chatting until the very last minute.

Walking down the aisle

Traditionally, the bride's father 'gives her away' by walking her down the aisle to the groom, but you needn't feel you have to do it this way. If your father has passed away or is not involved in your life, you could ask your mother, brother or stepfather. Some brides ask both parents to do the honours; others walk down the aisle with their own children. Some couples choose to walk down the aisle together.

Siobhan, Co Galway

At first I wasn't keen for my dad to walk me down the aisle – I felt like I was being treated as a piece of property to be passed on to my husband. But I really didn't want to disappoint my dad; I knew he would be so proud. In the end, I asked both my parents, which made it feel as if they were there to support me, rather than give me away.

You also need to decide whether you want the bridesmaids to walk down before you or after you. At Irish weddings, it's usually before. If you have flower girls or page boys, they also go on ahead, usually before the bridesmaids.

Lighting of the Candles

Catholic weddings begin with each of you lighting a candle to signify that you have come to the church as an individual. After the vows, you light the marriage candle together from the flames of these candles to signify your union in matrimony. You can buy candles from gift shops, larger card shops or religious bookshops. You can also get personalised candles, which are lovely but obviously more expensive. Or, if you still have your baptismal candles, it would be a lovely touch to use these.

Other Christian weddings don't normally include the lighting of candles, except when one of the couple is Catholic, when it's often incorporated.

Alvina, Wicklow

My husband and I met when we were both working as volunteers in Lourdes, and he proposed to me at the Grotto. For our wedding mass we chose to light our wedding candles on a separate altar dedicated to Our Lady, as we felt she had played a huge part in bringing us together.

THE READINGS

For the main Christian churches, it is usual to have one reading from the Old Testament, one from the New Testament and then the Gospel. These are some of the most popular readings for weddings:

Old Testament

Genesis 1:26-28.31 *Male and female he created them*
Tobit 8:4-8 *Grant that ... we may grow old together*
Song of Songs 2:8-10, 14, 16 *Arise, my love, my fair one, and come away*
Isaiah 61:10-11 *A bride adorns herself with jewels*
Ruth 1: *Wherever you go, I will go*
Jeremiah 31:31-34 *I will make a new covenant*

New Testament

Romans 8:31-35, 37, 39 *With God on our side, who can be against us?*

Romans 12:1-2, 9-18 *Let your love be genuine, and sincerely prefer good to evil*

Corinthians 12:31-13:8 *Love is always patient and kind*

Colossians 3:12-17 *Clothe yourselves with love*

Ephesians 3:14-21 *Being grounded in love*

John 3:18-24 *Let us love ... in truth and action*

Gospel

John 2:1-11 *The Wedding Feast at Cana*

John 15:9-12 *Abide in my love*

John 15:12-16 *Love one another*

Mark 10:6-9 *What God has joined together let no man put asunder*

Matthew 5:1-12 *The Beatitudes* [Blessed are the poor in spirit etc]

Matthew 22:35-42 *Love your neighbour as yourself*

You don't have to limit your choice to readings that relate to marriage. Put a bit of thought into it, and choose readings that mean something to you as a couple. It's worth explaining to the celebrant why you've chosen particular readings, as he or she might want to work it into the homily (sermon).

Only readings from Scripture can be used during the main part of the ceremony; your celebrant will have all the necessary Bible readings. If you'd like to include another reading, check with the celebrant if you could have it after communion, during the signing of the register, or if it could be included in the homily.

Readings for civil weddings

Choose your readings from your favourite poetry, prose, song lyrics, or even extracts from favourite films. Kahlil Gibran's 'The Prophet' and the love sonnets of Shakespeare are always popular. You could also consider:

- ♥ The poetry of Yeats, Keats or Elizabeth Barrett Browning
- ♥ The extract on the meaning of love in *Captain Corelli's Mandolin*
- ♥ 'Marriage Joins Two People in the Circle of Love' (Edmund O'Neil)
- ♥ 'A Gift from the Sea' (Anne Morrow Lindbergh)
- ♥ Eskimo love song
- ♥ Apache wedding blessing
- ♥ Irish blessing: 'May the road rise to meet you …'

Check out your local library for poetry collections. For wedding readings generally, search the internet. Sites such as www.hitched.co.uk and www.confetti.co.uk are good sources.

Don't be afraid to go for something a little out of the ordinary; a piece you can both really relate to will be much more moving than one of the more common readings.

Celebrity Style

When Paul McCartney married Heather Mills, Ringo Starr read a poem loosely based on the lyrics to 'All You Need is Love' – one of Paul's favourite Beatles songs.

Choosing readers

Choose your readers with care. It's important that the congregation be able to hear and understand the reading you have put so much thought into selecting. There's nothing more cringeworthy than hearing someone stumble through a reading, robbing it of all its meaning. It must also be pretty embarrassing for the person doing the reading, who may not have wanted to hurt you by turning down your request, but isn't really comfortable about it. Make sure you pick someone with a good speaking voice and the confidence to read what can be quite tricky language in front of a large number of people. If you really want to involve someone close to you but whom you know isn't ideal for the job, consider asking them to do a Prayer of the Faithful instead.

Make sure you give the chosen pieces to your readers a few weeks in advance so they have a chance to practise.

THE VOWS

For church weddings, you have to choose from the standard vows. In the Catholic church you have a choice of four – in three of these you get to say all the nice 'For better, for worse' bits, and in the fourth the priest says it for you and you just say 'I do'. The full wording of each option can be found on www.gettingmarried.ie. It's up to you which you go for, but personally I would advise against going for the last option – it makes your vows much more real if you say each phrase yourself and really think about what you're promising. In the Church of Ireland, you can choose between the traditional and modern versions of the solemnisation of marriage, which you can get from your minister. Within each of these is the option for the bride to promise to obey her husband; unsurprisingly, not many do these days. For civil weddings you need to incorporate certain words into your vows to fulfil the legal requirements. Wherever you're getting married, ask the celebrant what your options are.

To make your guests feel more involved, you could stand and face each other while you say your vows, or even turn and face the congregation. However, if you're shy, the best option is probably the traditional one, where the bride and groom face the celebrant. Whichever option you choose, make sure to speak slowly and clearly so the guests can hear your vows. If it's a big church, use a microphone.

Celebrity Style

When Jennifer Aniston married Brad Pitt, she promised to make his 'favourite banana milkshake' and he vowed to 'split the difference on the thermostat'.

EXCHANGE OF THE RINGS

The vows are followed by the exchange of rings (with a blessing in the case of a church wedding). Again, you can choose between different forms of words. It goes without saying that the groom should check at least twelve times that the best man has the rings safely in his pocket! (Remember the ring chaos in *Four Weddings and a Funeral?*)

Lorraine, Laois

My mother's best friend made our ring cushion with our initials in Mountmellick embroidery. She left space on it so that our children's initials can be embroidered onto it when they are getting married, so I guess it will become a family heirloom!

Does the groom have to wear a wedding ring?

Only a generation ago many, if not most men never wore a wedding ring. Today that's much more unusual. While a lot of men are a bit reluctant at first because they might not normally wear jewellery, most decide to get a wedding ring and often end up loving it. Others are firmly opposed to the idea.

If your husband-to-be really doesn't want to wear a ring, maybe you're fine with that. Some brides threaten that they won't wear a wedding ring unless he does (this has been known to result in instant success in an astonishing number of cases). Or they tell him that they'll change their name to his if he wears his ring – it's all part of the being married deal. If you feel that this is unfair pressure, you could try a compromise: maybe he could just wear the ring when you go out in the evenings (many men who work with their hands choose this option as more practical anyway).

Even if he's not going to wear a ring, many grooms choose to get one anyway for the wedding day, as it's a lovely symbolic part of the ceremony.

Exchange of gifts between bride and groom (Catholic weddings)

Traditionally, the groom gave the bride a coin to represent the fact that all his property was now hers too. Nowadays, if you choose to include this in the ceremony, the bride usually gives the groom a coin also. You can buy wedding coins from jewellers; some jewellers supply the coin free when you buy your rings. You could also consider giving another gift, such as jewellery, or a token that represents something important to you both.

It's nice to give something old, like a silver crown or half-crown, or a specially minted coin, like the Irish Silver £1 Millennium coin. A medal representing a sporting or other achievement, such as an All Ireland medal, would also be special.

The tokens are exchanged with the words: 'I give you this gift as a token of all I possess.'

PRAYERS (OF THE FAITHFUL)

You can write your own Prayers of the Faithful (simply Prayers in the Church of Ireland), ask the celebrant's help to write them, or adapt them from prayers used by others or general prayers that the celebrant provides.

Take the opportunity to personalise them. For example, if someone you love and who would have been part of your wedding – a parent/grandparent/ sibling – has passed away, remember them; if someone close is ill or abroad and can't make it, remember them and all patients/ emigrants; if you have a particular cause you believe in, mention it. You can get many family and friends involved in reading the prayers.

SIGNING THE REGISTER

Either before or after the final blessing, the bride and groom and the two witnesses (sometimes accompanied by others from the bridal party, including parents) go into the sacristy, or perhaps to a side altar, to sign the marriage register. Remember to sign the register in your maiden name, even if you intend to change it.

Then, you and your new husband lead the procession back up the aisle to the applause of your guests. Traditionally, the best man walks out with the chief bridesmaid, the groomsmen with other bridesmaids, the groom's father with the bride's mother, and the bride's father with the groom's mother.

CHOOSING YOUR MUSIC

Religious ceremonies

Churches tend to be fairly strict about what music can be played at weddings. Some clergy won't allow any non-religious music. Even the Bridal March (Here Comes the Bride) is not allowed in many Catholic churches because it's not actually a religious piece. Others will allow you to have non-religious music as long as it's only instrumental and the lyrics aren't sung. Some will allow a non-religious piece to be played at the signing of the register, as the religious part of the ceremony is over at this point. Check with the clergy in your chosen church before proceeding.

The Dublin Diocesan Liturgical Resource Centre has compiled an album of twenty-six tracks considered 'appropriate' for church weddings. 'The Wedding Album' is available on CD from Veritas and other bookshops and record stores.

One of the problems with selecting wedding music is that while you can probably hum a few bars of what you have in mind, you don't have a clue what it's called. Your best bet is to listen to music online on sites such as www.webwedding.co.uk/article/music or to invest in a CD or two of wedding music – these can be hard to find in shops but you should have no trouble buying them from www.amazon.co.uk. 'Beautiful Wedding Melodies' and 'Wedding Music' are two I've come across. Have a look in your local music store at collections from such as Luciano Pavarotti, Kiri Te Kanawa and Andrea Bocelli for classics like 'Ave Maria' and 'Panis Angelicus'.

You should also think about what music is normally played at ordinary church services; much of it would be perfectly appropriate for weddings also. Best of all, ask the advice of your musicians and get them to play/sing a bit of the pieces they recommend.

Fionnuala, Dublin

My husband has always loved Russia and all things Russian. As a special surprise on our wedding day, I asked the organist to play the Russian national anthem while we were signing the register. The look of amazement and delight on his face said it all!

Some of the popular music choices for different parts of the ceremony:

Processional:

Canon in D (Pachelbel)
Bridal March [Here Comes the Bride] (Wagner)
Mozart's Wedding March (from the Marriage of Figaro)
Arrival of the Queen of Sheba (Handel)
Jesu, Joy of Man's Desiring (Bach)
Hornpipe (Handel)
Trumpet Theme from Te Deum (Charpentier)
Ode to Joy (Beethoven)

Lighting of the candles (Catholic):

Canon in D (Pachelbel)
Jesu, Joy of Man's Desiring (Bach)
Carolan's Air (Carolan)
Gabriel's Oboe (Morricone)
One Hand, One Heart (Bernstein)
Ave Maria (Schubert/Bach/Gounod)

Opening Hymn (Church of Ireland):

O Christ who once hast deigned
O Perfect Love
Be thou my vision
Here I am Lord
(see additional hymns, page 112)

Psalm:

Song of Ruth
May your Love be upon us

On Eagle's Wings
Here I am Lord
Sé an Tiarna m'Aoire
The Lord's My Shepherd

Lighting of marriage candle (Catholic):

Canon in D (Pachelbel)
Air on a G string (Bach)
One Hand, One Heart (Bernstein)

Offertory (Catholic):

Ave Maria (Schubert/Bach/Gounod)
Ag Críost an Síol
Bí Iosa im Chroíse
As I Kneel Before you
Agnus Dei from Coronation Mass (Mozart)

Communion:

Panis Angelicus (Franck)
Laudate Dominum (Mozart)
Close to You
Ag Críost an Síol
One Bread, One Body
Take and Eat

Signing the Register:

Eine Kleine Nachtmusik (Mozart)
Ode to Joy (Beethoven)
Trumpet Tune (Purcell)
Flower Duet from Lackme (Delibes)
Romance from The Gadfly (Shostakovich)

Recessional:

Arrival of the Queen of Sheba (Handel)

Wedding March from A Midsummer Night's Dream (Mendelssohn)

Spring from the Four Seasons (Vivaldi)

Laudate Dominum (Mozart)

Note: For Church of Ireland weddings, the congregation normally joins in the singing so it's important to choose hymns people will be familiar with. It's also worth including the words in your wedding booklet. Here are some of the most popular:

All Things Bright and Beautiful

Love is his word

One more step along the world I go

Morning has broken

Amazing Grace

Make me a channel of your peace

Brother, sister, let me serve you

How Great Thou Art

For the Beauty of the Earth

O Perfect Love

Music for civil ceremonies

For civil weddings, you have a much broader scope of music to choose from. You might want to stay within the classical wedding genre, or you might go with your favourite love songs. At least you won't have to worry about a priest banning you from playing Westlife (though you may have to worry about your friends laughing at your taste). Although some registry offices don't have room (or time) for musicians, you can play CDs, so give someone the job of pressing play at the right moment.

WEDDING BOOKLETS

Your wedding booklet (often known as the order of service or Mass booklet) helps the guests to follow what's happening during the ceremony and is a lovely souvenir of the day, both for them and for you. Keep the booklets from any weddings you or your families attend before your wedding. They'll give you ideas for readings and music as well as the general structure of the service.

If you know anyone who got married recently, ask them to e-mail you their wedding booklet. You can use it as a template and adapt it to your own needs – it'll save you typing out lots of bits that remain the same. (There seem to be so many of these in circulation that it's probably years since anyone has actually created one from scratch).

You'll also find sample wedding booklets on www.simplyweddings.com.

You can begin preparing your booklet as early as you like; it can be quite a time-consuming job, so it's good to get it underway as soon as you've got an idea of your readings and music. You needn't finalise it until you're sure of your choices. It's also nice to include the names of those taking part in the ceremony: readers and singers as well as the bridal party.

Don't feel you have to include every single word that will be spoken at the service. It's better to keep it simple; in many cases just the headings will do e.g. Liturgy of the Eucharist, Blessing of the Rings etc. That way guests will be more inclined to watch what's happening rather than read it. If your guests are not regular attendees in whichever denomination church you are getting married, it might be wise to include the instructions: All Rise, Kneel, Stand, so that no one is embarrassed by not knowing what to do. One bride I know had to write out these instructions for her groom – but that's another story!

For a simpler version of the wedding booklet, why not use a scroll instead – an A4 sheet printed on both sides, rolled up and tied with ribbon. It will obviously hold less information, but it's far easier to do, uses less paper and requires very little assembly. Bear in mind that scrolls can create a bit of noise in the church when guests start to unroll them, so go for a paper that isn't too stiff.

Be sure to ask the celebrant to check the booklet before you print it. You should also ask someone with a good eye for detail to check spelling, grammar and punctuation – typing mistakes could really spoil the effect of your beautiful creation.

If you're getting the booklets printed along with your invitations and other stationery (*see* Chapter 9), be sure to allow plenty of time.

A FEW MORE NOTES ON CHURCH WEDDINGS

Inviting the celebrant to the reception

The normal practice is to invite your celebrant to the wedding reception also. Unless they're friends of the family they probably won't go, or might just go to the meal and leave afterwards, but it's nice to invite them anyway, as they're such an important part of your day.

The sacristan

The sacristan is the person who opens the church in the mornings and takes care of heating, lighting and so on. Couples usually give him or her a small fee as a thank-you. If you're unsure how much to give, ask the clergy what's usually done.

Altar servers

You might like to include children of relatives or friends as altar servers, assuming they know what to do – check if the celebrant is happy with this. If you don't have anyone you want to use, the celebrant will organise it for you. It's usual to give them a small amount of money as a thank-you.

Photography

Check that the church allows photography and video recording. Some clergy take the view that it interferes with the solemnity of the occasion, though most won't mind if it's done discreetly.

Confetti

Confetti is very rarely used these days – it creates litter in the church grounds – and rice, which was a common alternative, is hazardous to birds, as it swells in their stomachs after they eat it, so it is also frowned upon. If you really want confetti, check with your celebrant that it's permitted. You might also consider more environmentally friendly options such as biodegradable rose petals. Another alternative is to distribute bubbles for guests to blow as you leave the church – make sure they won't stain your dress.

If you do use confetti or some other material that needs to

be cleaned up afterwards, there may be an extra fee involved.

Rehearsal

The rehearsal is usually held in the week before the wedding, sometimes as late as the day before, if some of the bridal party are coming from out of town. *See* Chapter 10.

CHAPTER SEVEN

Cakes and Cars, Flowers and Photos

N ow that you have settled on your date and time, booked a venue for the ceremony and reception, and set in train the legal requirements, it's time to concentrate on assembling all the other ingredients that will make your big day special.

Do your homework first; sourcing wedding suppliers can be a bit daunting and you can easily be swayed into having something that you're not happy with if you haven't already got a clear idea of what you do and don't want. So, go through magazines and search the internet to get an idea of what you want before you start looking. There are numerous bridal magazines to choose from, but bear in mind that the

Irish-published ones will have the most relevant information for Irish weddings: locations, suppliers etc.

Wedding fairs are great places to find suppliers. You can meet dozens under one roof, have a look through their catalogues, and ask them any questions you have in mind. The biggest fairs are probably those held annually in Dublin, either at the Point or in the RDS in Ballsbridge, so look out for these, but there are wedding fairs held in hotels up and down the country, where all the local suppliers will have displays – check with your hotel whether they have one coming up.

Talk to as many past brides as you can, and get their feedback. If you don't know many personally, some of the suppliers in whom you're interested may be willing to put you in touch with a few of their recent customers for a recommendation.

Decide what your priorities are, and plan to spend most time on those. If you're not particularly interested in the cake, there's no point in giving it too much time and attention – make a quick decision and cross it off your list.

PHOTOGRAPHER

Many couples rate the choice of photographer as second only to the choice of venue, requiring the most thought and consideration, and indeed money.

Your wedding album is something you will treasure for years to come. If you have children, they'll love taking it out to see how Mammy and Daddy looked on that very special day, even if, as they get older, it may only be to laugh at the hairstyles and out-of-date fashions of the guests! If you'll let her, your mum will proudly show it off to everyone she knows. Your friends will ask to see it at every party you host for the next year at least. And most of all, you and your husband will love flicking through it and bringing back all those happy memories of the day your marriage began.

Start looking for a photographer as early as you can. A photographer can do only one wedding a day, and they are often booked up two years or more in advance. Having said that, if you're planning your wedding in a short timeframe, don't despair – often photographers just happen to have dates free, and weekdays in particular are less likely to be booked up.

Have a look at different styles of wedding photography and decide what's best for you: traditional, classical, contemporary, posed, relaxed are just some of the ranges on offer. Traditional wedding photos are posed and formal, consisting of group shots of families and portrait-style shots of the bride and groom. Reportage photography is, as the name suggests, a more candid and informal style that captures the story and atmosphere of the day.

Often the style of the wedding you are planning will influence the type of photography that will be suitable – a large, formal wedding will probably demand a more traditional style of photography, while for a simpler wedding a more spontaneous style of photography would be more appropriate.

Most couples like to get a mixture of styles. You need some traditional posed photos to make sure you have shots of all your family, a record of who was there and what they were wearing. But reportage photos mean you don't miss out on wonderful moments like your little nephew falling asleep in his dad's arms or your mum shedding a tear as you walk down the aisle. Many photographers will also do both black and white and colour photos, so you can have a mixture.

Get recommendations from family and friends, check the discussion boards on websites, and the Irish Professional Photographers website, www.irishphotographers.com.

Céara, Co Galway

My father-in-law paid for our photos as a wedding present. Instead of a conventional album, we decided to go for a Wedding Book, which contains 50 to 100 selected pictures presented using graphic design, digital print and bookbinding. It's personalised, with the names of the bride and groom printed inside. We were so excited to get our wedding book and astonished at how well it turned out. As well as our own copy, we got smaller books for our parents and pocket-sized versions for each of the bridal party. As the photographs were taken in both a reportage and portraiture style, we had to pose only for the shots we wanted with our families. The photographer trailed us for the rest of the day, taking shots that were ultimately combined into a storybook version of the whole day, from hair and make-up in the morning to our first dance after dinner.

Irish wedding magazines are a good source of information on photographers, as they often carry ads or features that show a selection of their work. And most, if not all, wedding photographers will have their own websites where you can view their work at your leisure. If there is a photographer's studio in your area, take a good look at the window display. If this is the work the photographer is proudest of and it is not to your taste, then he/she is probably not the one for you.

However, you don't have to confine your search to local photographers. Many are willing to travel to different parts of the country, although there is usually an extra charge for this.

Once you've done your initial research and got the names of some photographers who seem suitable in terms of both style and price, visit their studios to view sample albums, have a chat with them, and ask a few more questions. It's worth seeing at least two or three so you can be sure you have a good idea of the different options on offer. If your wedding is taking place in your home area and it's not practical for you to make these visits in person because you live too far away, ask someone whose opinion you value – your mother or your bridesmaid – to do this for you. But do try to double-check at some point yourself. You need to be sure you've found the style that's right for you and your wedding.

When looking at sample albums, here are some things to look out for:

- Are the photos clear, well-focused, colour accurate and professionally printed?
- Can you see all the detail on dresses and outfits and the expressions on people's faces?
- Is the background providing an attractive setting for the photos rather than distracting from the subjects?
- Does the album tell the story of the day from beginning to end in a simple but stylish way?
- Is there a good mixture of group shots, portrait shots and story shots?

As well as having a look at sample albums, you might want to ask some questions, such as:

💜 What types of album are available? Can you supply an album of your own choosing, and if so, will you get a discount on the total bill?

💜 Is there a set number of pictures in the finished album, or can extra pages be added?

💜 How long does the photographer spend with you on the day?

💜 How long will the photographer spend taking posed pictures?

💜 What kinds of extras are available? These can include albums for your parents, smaller keepsake albums for the bridal party, framed photos and thank you cards

💜 Will they put your wedding photos on their website, or host a wedding gallery which your friends and family can view?

In terms of the length of time you want to spend with the photographer, think about what you'd like. Photographers will usually have a set routine, but they may be willing to vary it for an extra charge. For example, their usual pattern might be to start at the bride's house as she gets ready, photograph the ceremony and the aftermath, and finish up with a photo of the couple cutting the cake (these are often faked, rather than having the photographer hang around waiting for the real cutting). But if you want them to stay on to take photos of your first dance, they may do so for an extra charge. This may also mean you will have to provide a meal for them.

At a set time, usually between the ceremony and the meal, the photographer will take shots of the families and bridal party; alternatively, he may shoot the couple on their own in a scenic location nearby, or in the hotel garden if there is one. This does mean that the bride and groom are late joining their own party, but most feel that it's worth it to have a stylish record of their day. The amount of time the photographer expects you to spend on photo shoots can vary quite a bit, and you should think about how much time you're willing to devote.

It's also important that you personally meet the photographer who will be taking the photos on the day. You need to feel at ease with this person, to trust that they will add to the enjoyment of the day rather than take from it, will be unobtrusive, and will be able to gather people together for formal shots without being bossy or taking over. Have you ever noticed how you smile more naturally in photos when the person behind the camera is someone you like? You may think that on your wedding day no one will be able to stop you beaming from ear to ear, but you'd be surprised at how irritable you could become after a lengthy session of posing for photos for someone who is getting on your nerves.

At the end of the day much of the reason for choosing a photographer is instinct – you just instantly like the style of the sample albums or warm to the photographer's personality.

Once you've decided ...

Once you've chosen your photographer, pay a deposit to secure your date and get a written agreement outlining the terms of the arrangement.

You should also find out when you will get your proofs, if they will be hard copies or on CD or both, and how long it will take to get the album after you submit your order.

Nearer to the Big Day ...

Contact the photographer again to finalise all the details, such as where the bride is getting ready, what time the photographer should be there, what time the ceremony starts, where photos will be taken after the ceremony, what you will do if it rains, and what time the photographer will finish up. Also, find out when the photographer will need final payment.

Some people will tell you to give the photographer a list of must-take shots. In general I don't think this is really necessary. A professional photographer is not going to forget to capture things like the families, the bride with her attendants and the groom with his, or the signing of the register. This is their job and they know what they're doing. However, if you're very particular about this, by all means do up a list and give it to the photographer in good time – it may help set your mind at ease. And you should definitely give notice in advance if there is something out of the ordinary you want photographed – perhaps a shot of you with all your college friends, or something along those lines.

Budget Ideas

If you are on a very tight budget or if photos are simply not your priority, ask a trusted friend with a good camera to be your photographer for the day. Give them a list of must-take shots. As a back-up, ask other guests if you can borrow their negatives to make copies. You could even mention in the note that you enclose with the invitations that you're not having a photographer and would appreciate if guests could send you copies of their best photos. Arrange to have disposable cameras on guests' tables and encourage them to take photos of the various groups, the dancing etc. Delegate someone to collect these cameras at the end of the day and to arrange for processing the film while you are on honeymoon.

Beat The Stress

Have nothing to do with any suppliers who are inconsiderate, rude, or difficult to deal with. Make the break early rather than late; you don't need the hassle. You are planning the happiest day of your life, and you don't have to put up with poor customer service.

VIDEOGRAPHER

Should we have a video?

While most couples wouldn't dream of doing without a professional photographer, feelings will probably be a lot more mixed about the issue of a video/DVD. We're all used to having our photo taken at parties, picnics and when someone has a film they want to use up, but having your every move captured on video is another matter. Many brides are torn between wanting to have a record of all the best moments of the day, and being afraid that the camera will make them feel self-conscious and interfere with the guests' enjoyment.

Professional videographers will tell you that they blend into the background, and won't even be noticed, and to a certain extent that's true. Nowadays there is no need for the glaring white lights or elaborate equipment that used to be associated with wedding videos. However, some people – both bridal party and guests – are still going to be uncomfortably aware that they're on camera and may not be able to fully relax and enjoy the day.

I have to admit to a certain prejudice here. I didn't have a wedding video and have never once regretted it. For me, the photographs are a much nicer record of the day. Having had to endure watching myself on other people's videos either propping up the bar for hours on end or trying to find a corner of the dance floor out of reach of the lens, I didn't want to inflict that on either myself or my guests – much to the relief of my husband. My bridesmaids felt the same way and one assured me afterwards that she wouldn't have worn out the soles of her dancing shoes half as fast if there had been a camera pointed at her. But most importantly to me, I prefer to remember the wedding as I saw it and not as the camera did.

However, I do have lots of friends who are delighted they had their wedding videoed, and always watch it again on anniversaries and other special days. The day goes by so fast that it's nice to be able to watch it all again at your leisure. It's particularly good to be able to see parts of the day you might

Paula, Cork

Watching the video for the first time was an amazing experience, reliving the day again and seeing how happy we both were. It was also great seeing everyone enjoying themselves. Some of my aunts in London weren't able to make the wedding so we sent them a copy and they were delighted that they got to see it. They had seen photos but they felt they were able to experience the day themselves by watching the video. And in years to come it will be great showing our children our wedding day.

have missed, such as guests arriving at the church, and you can look forward to being able to show the video/DVD to your children. And none of these friends have ever made me sit through three hours of their wedding video (surely on a par with viewing someone else's holiday slides), which is why they are still my friends.

As a compromise, you could ask a friend or relative with a decent camcorder to record the most important moments of the day, such as the ceremony and speeches. Just be prepared for the fact that the quality will not be as good, and that amateurs are a lot more likely to forget to charge batteries or get distracted into filming a fist fight between the flower girl and page boy instead of your vows.

If you do decide to hire a professional videographer, take the time to ensure you are getting the right person for the job. Get recommendations from friends and borrow their videos (you can fast-forward the boring bits). Select two or three potential videographers and ask for a demo tape to view at home. It's one thing to watch a selection of their best shots on professional equipment in a studio, but what you really want to know is how it will look on your video or DVD player at home.

When viewing a demo, some of the things you should look out for are:

♥ Are the images properly in focus?

♥ Is there too much camera movement, zooming or wobbling?

♥ Is the colour even and accurate?

♥ Is the sound clear?

♥ Has the editing been skilfully done, or are there too many dull moments left in, or lots of disconcerting switching of scenes?

You should also ask about the music that will be used for background – some videographers will let you supply your own. Find out if they can give you a copy on DVD as well (or instead).

Make sure you meet the person who will be doing your video on the day. As with the photographer, it's important that you get on well with them and feel comfortable in their company.

Once you've decided …

Pay a deposit to secure your date, and get a receipt confirming both the amount and the wedding date.

Nearer to the Big Day …

Meet with the videographer again and run through any particular concerns you have. Remember, it's your day and their job is to capture it the way you want it.

If you have anything special planned for the ceremony or reception, make sure to tell them in advance so they're prepared for it.

And if you're worried that your guests won't enjoy the dancing if they're being filmed, or that your Hollywood romantic movie will deteriorate into a scene at the Queen Vic as the night goes on, then just ask the videographer to finish recording after the first dance.

FLORIST

In terms of prioritising your planning, choosing a florist is not something on which I would recommend spending too much time. In smaller towns, your family probably has a relationship with a local florist over the years, and if you're happy with their level of service and the price they quote you for a wedding package, there's probably not much need for shopping around.

Otherwise, again get some recommendations from family, friends and your church or wedding venue. Particularly in the case of churches, it's useful if the florist has handled weddings there before, as they will know how many arrangements are needed and what the routine is for putting them in place and removing them afterwards if necessary.

What you're really looking for in a florist is someone who is polite, helpful, has lots of good ideas, a good eye for matching flowers to styles and colours of dresses, and enthusiasm for your day. And of course, someone who won't charge you the earth.

Once you've decided...

Pay a deposit to secure your date, and find out when they want you to come back to choose your flowers.

CHOOSING THE FLOWERS

Choosing the flowers, as opposed to the florist, takes a bit more time and planning. Any time between four weeks and four months before the wedding, meet the florist to decide what flowers you want. You should bring a photo of your dress and the bridesmaid dresses, and ideally fabric swatches of both.

Before you meet, have an idea of the type of flowers you would like and the preferred shape of the bouquets for yourself and your bridesmaids. There is a magazine called *Wedding Flowers* which is published once a year and has a wonderful range of photos of flowers of every kind. It's usually available in spring. You'll also find plenty of photos in ordinary wedding magazines and on the net – some useful sites are www.theknot.com and www.marthastewart.com – both American, but flowers are not very different over there! Bring along any cuttings or printouts that you think would work. The florist will also have brochures or albums you can look through.

For the bride's bouquet, some of the most popular styles are:

♥ An inverted teardrop or shower bouquet, suitable for most kinds of flowers; it is usually mixed with a lot of greenery, which gives a cascading impression and highlights the flow of the bride's dress. Most traditional but still very popular

♥ A compact, round posy, most commonly seen with roses or tulips. This is a formal but very modern style

♥ A hand-tied, loose posy, probably tied with ribbon. This is a more relaxed and contemporary style

♥ A tall sheaf of flowers, such as arum lilies, usually carried in your arms as you would hold a baby rather than clasped in your hands. Another very modern, simple, stylish bouquet.

You should take into account the style of the wedding overall, the style and shape of your dress, your own height and build, and the colour of the bridesmaid dresses. If you're not sure, the florist will be able to help you decide what would look best.

Choose flowers that will be in season at the time of your wedding, as this works out much cheaper. Some brides select certain flowers for their bouquets because of their symbolic meaning: Chrysanthemums for truth, ferns for sincerity, freesias for friendship, gypsophila [baby's breath] or heather for good luck, ivy for a long-lasting marriage, and myrtle because of its association with Venus, the Goddess of Love.

THE MEANING OF FLOWERS

Almond blossom	Hope
Amaryllis	Pride
Apple blossom	Perfection
Arum lily	Ardour
Azalea	True to the end
Bluebell	Everlasting love
Carnation	Woman in love
Chrysanthemum	Truth
Daisy	Innocence
Fern	Sincerity
Forget-me-not	True love
Freesia	Friendship
Gypsophila	Good luck
Holly	Domestic happiness
Heather	Good luck
Iris	Friendship
Ivy	Fidelity/long-lasting marriage
Jonquil	Desire
Lilac	Love
Lily	Purity
Lily of the valley	Happiness
Marigold	Constancy
Myrtle	Love
Orchid	Beauty
Rose	Romance or pleasure
Snowdrop	Hope
Stephanotis	Travel

Sunflower	Adoration
Sweet pea	Lasting pleasure
Sweet William	A smile
Tulip	Declaration of love
Violets	Modesty and faithfulness

Check that no one in the bridal party is allergic to particular flowers or suffers from hay fever. Check that the fragrance of the flowers won't be too overwhelming.

These are some of the items you might want to order:

♥ Bride's bouquet

♥ Bridesmaids' bouquets

♥ Flower girls' posies or baskets

♥ Buttonholes for the groom, best man, groomsmen, fathers of the bride and groom, and any other special male guests such as brothers or grandfathers of the bride and groom. (For very elaborate weddings, buttonholes are sometimes ordered for the entire congregation, but this is very expensive and certainly not expected)

♥ Corsages for the mothers of the bride and groom, and any other special female guests, such as sisters or grandmothers of the bride and groom (these can be either pinned to outfits or attached to handbags)

♥ Arrangements for the church

♥ Arrangements for the reception

♥ Centrepieces for the reception

♥ Any presentation bouquets, such as to the mothers.

The custom of men wearing buttonholes stems from the early days of jousting, when a Knight would wear his Lady's colours during the contest to symbolise his love for her.

A Little Bit of History

Nearer to the Big Day ...

Find out if the florist is going to deliver the flowers for the bridal party to your home and at what time. Don't forget that the buttonholes will have to be delivered to wherever the groom is staying – if the florist isn't going to do this, assign the job to a helpful family member.

Budget Ideas

To save money and get maximum use from your flowers, you could bring the arrangements from the church to the reception. Just be careful that this doesn't offend the clergy; it might be best to leave at least one arrangement in the church. The florist should be able to tell you what's normally done.

Another money-saving tip is to find out if there is another wedding in the church on the same day and see if the other couple would be willing to share the same flowers and split the cost. This of course depends on you having similar taste and colour schemes, or sticking to something simple like all white flowers and greenery.

Before you decide to order expensive centrepieces or other arrangements for the reception venue, check if they supply their own. Hotels often provide simple flower arrangements and may even tie these in with your colour scheme. Or you may want to consider different table arrangements – *see* Chapter 12.

Do your own

If you are good with your hands, and you have the time, why not do your own flowers, and get your bridesmaids or family members to help? You can buy flowers cheaply at markets on the day before the wedding and arrange them into simple, pretty bouquets and buttonholes. A florist will sell you florist's wire and ribbon if you need it.

> *Niamh, Sligo*
>
> My bridesmaid and I did the flowers for the whole wedding party. I bought florist's wire and tape from a florist, and ribbon and muslin from the fabric shop. We bought three bunches of mixed flowers in the supermarket the day before the wedding, and spent the afternoon arranging them into bouquets. My bouquet was wrapped in muslin and purple ribbon to match the bridesmaid dress. It saved us a few hundred euro, and it's lovely seeing my own handiwork in the photos!

Alternatives

Instead of flowers, have your bridesmaids carry candles down the aisle – this is particularly effective for winter weddings.

You could also consider artificial flowers, dried flowers or silk flowers – these can work out much cheaper, especially from companies who simply hire them out to you. And you won't have to worry about wilting flowers or hay fever.

If it's a Christmas wedding, why not have a berry and ivy theme? Holly and ivy will only cost the time it takes to collect them, and they can make very effective end-of-pew and window decorations in churches, with a big festive arrangement outside the church door, easily arranged in a container of oasis.

TRANSPORT

You want to arrive at the church in style, so just how are you going to do it? The most popular modes of transport are limousines or vintage cars such as Rolls Royces. For the real fairytale feel, you could hire a horse and carriage and be a princess for the day. Or if money's no object, how about a helicopter to whisk you and your new husband off to your reception, assuming that your venues have the necessary safety clearance for this. It will certainly make a statement – just be careful of that hairdo!

Again, recommendations from other brides, your venue, and contacts made at wedding fairs are good sources of information. Think about the type of car that would suit the style of your wedding, and go to see a few suppliers.

Consider what the car or cars are required for: you need to get you, your parents and your bridesmaids to the church, and you and your new husband to the reception. If you live close enough to the church, the car could make two trips, first bringing the bridesmaids to the church, then returning for you and your father. Your mother can travel either with the bridesmaids or with you.

The best man is normally responsible for driving the groom to the church. Afterwards, he should drive the bridesmaids to the reception, or to where photos are being taken.

At the risk of sounding very sexist, organising the transport is a good way to get a disinterested groom involved. You could delegate the job to him entirely, leaving you with one less thing to worry about, or you could have a fun afternoon investigating the options together.

Remember to consider the size of your dress. Unless it's a very svelte number, you'll need lots of legroom to prevent it getting squashed and creased.

Your husband-to-be will probably think you are completely daft when you mention this to him, but don't forget your colour scheme when looking at cars – a red Mercedes may be your ideal wedding car, but bridesmaids emerging from it in candy pink frocks might look a bit garish in your photos.

You might also consider hiring a wedding bus or smaller coach for some of your guests. It means that everyone who wants to can have a few drinks and no one will have to be the teetotal 'designated driver'.

Once you've chosen ...

Pay a deposit and get a receipt confirming the date and time of the wedding.

Nearer to the Big Day ...

Ring the driver to re-confirm the booking. Give him directions to where you'll be getting ready and what time you want him to be there. Always err on the side of caution; ask him to be there at least half an hour before you need to leave. Let him know if you've made any arrangement with the photographer to go somewhere for photos after the ceremony. Find out if the driver carries umbrellas in case it rains, or if you should bring your own.

Budget

If you don't want the expense of a wedding car, ask a friend or relation with a nice car to drive you to the church. Or have someone hire a fancy car for the weekend and be your chauffeur. This could be their wedding present to you.

CAKE

This can be a fun part of the wedding planning, especially if you get to taste lots of samples. Your wedding cake can be as elaborate or as simple as you like, decorated with flowers, feathers, ribbons, hearts, stars or almost anything that takes your fancy.

The cake at Irish weddings was traditionally a rich fruit cake, and fruit cake does have advantages: it keeps very well and you can hold on to the top tier if you want to adhere to the custom of using it for the christening party of your first child. However, most couples nowadays chose a variety of cakes to form the various tiers: chocolate, madeira, carrot, chocolate biscuit, lemon. It's really a matter of personal taste, and you can still have one tier of fruitcake if you wish.

Cakemakers have let their imaginations run wild in recent years, as you'll soon see when you flick through their files. You can get cakes made up in the shape of your church, a car, a ship, a pile of hat boxes or suitcases, or in the shape of your favourite cartoon characters. Ours was a fairytale castle and was a real focal point at the reception.

If you want the effect of lots of tiers but can't afford or don't need that many, the cakemaker should be able to provide a few false tiers – cardboard boxes decorated with icing – to create the look.

Breda, Co Cork

I had always hated fruitcake, so was determined not to have it for my wedding cake. Instead, I had a three-tiered cake made entirely of ice cream. It looked exactly like a traditional cake, with smooth white ice cream 'icing', piping and yellow flowers. Obviously, it couldn't be left out of the freezer too long, but we went through the usual 'cutting of the cake' ritual and no one was any the wiser. The ice cream was duly served to the guests in wedges at the end of the meal. I heard later that some of the older aunts had enjoyed the dessert but couldn't understand why they had got no cake! What kind of a wedding was it at all?

Once you've chosen ...

Pay a deposit and find out when you need to confirm exactly what you want.

Nearer to the Big Day ...

Confirm the kind(s) of cake you want and how many people it needs to feed. Make arrangements to have the cake delivered to the hotel. If the cakemaker hasn't dealt with your hotel before, give them the necessary contact details.

Budget

Ask a friend or relation to bake the cake for you or have a go at it yourself if you feel competent to do this. If you are sticking with the traditional fruitcake, it's no more difficult to make than a Christmas cake. Unfortunately it's still quite expensive to get a cake iced even if you provide it yourself, so if your helper isn't experienced at this, just get them to finish it off with simple white icing or white fondant icing that can be rolled out like pastry and smoothed over the shape of the cake. You can have fun decorating it yourself with flowers or whatever takes your fancy.

You can get readymade simple wedding cakes in some stores, eg Marks and Spencer. They even provide the little pillars so you can have tiers.

THE MUSIC

The music for your wedding day deserves a lot of thought. From the moment you walk down the aisle, through the ceremony, at the reception, and later in the evening for the dancing, it will set the mood, re-inforce the message of love and union that is the theme of your wedding, and put the unique stamp of your personalities on the whole day.

Ceremony

For a church wedding, you will need to talk to the celebrant about the choice of music. (*See* Chapter 6 in relation to music allowed in churches). The celebrant should be able to put you in touch with the regular organist, who will, in turn, have some suggestions for soloists or choirs with whom they have worked previously. The celebrant may also suggest a folk choir, or other musicians such as a harpist or string quartet.

Try to hear the suggested musicians in performance before making your choice. If you don't want to go for the resident organist/musician, you will need to check with the celebrant whether it's OK to bring in someone else. It is well established practice that where a church professionally employs an organist, he/she is normally entitled to receive a 'displacement' fee when the couple wish to use an organist of their own choice. Guidelines on fees for church musicians have been drawn up by the Catholic and Church of Ireland churches, so you will be able to get guidance on the appropriate fees from your clergy.

Once you've chosen ...

Find out if a deposit is required – musicians are often more laidback about this than other wedding suppliers.

Nearer the Big Day ...

Meet the organist/musicians to decide how many pieces you want performed during the ceremony, and choose a list of suitable music – *see* Chapter 6 for suggestions.

The drinks reception

Consider asking your church musicians if they will play for an hour or two at your drinks reception – it could work out relatively inexpensive, although you may have to arrange transport for them. This works particularly well with a harpist or string quartet. A jazz band, or a piper to serenade you into the reception room, are also very appropriate.

It's best to avoid having singers at this part of the day, as it's a distraction from conversation. At this time guests really get a chance to mingle, catch up with old friends and long lost cousins, and marvel at how gorgeous you look in your dress. You want the music to provide a pleasant backdrop to this, rather than dominating.

You don't have to have musicians for the drinks reception – perhaps the venue isn't really suitable, or guests will be wandering out to the gardens, or you just don't think it's necessary. The hotel will usually play CDs in the background anyway, or you could provide them with your own.

The meal

Some couples choose to have a pianist or harpist play during the meal. This is a nice touch, particularly at very formal weddings, but again isn't really necessary, as this is a time for conversation. Again, the hotel will usually play CDs at this point, and you could provide them with your own. Classical music or easy listening is best.

The evening

The formalities of the day are over and it's time to kick off those high heels and party! If the music at your reception gets everyone onto the floor, then this will be a huge contributory factor in your guests remembering your wedding as a 'great day'. Think about:

- ♥ The age of your guests and what their taste in music is likely to be
- ♥ Your own likes and dislikes
- ♥ The style of the wedding
- ♥ The size and shape of the reception room, both for dancing and for acoustics.

On the one hand, this is your chance to have all your favourite music played – you might never get another opportunity to decide on what all your friends and family will be dancing and singing along to. On the other hand, if your passion for heavy metal is not shared by the guests, then you will have the dance floor to yourself – not a recipe for success.

If yours has been a formal wedding so far, with lots of older family relatives, then your traditional wedding could be rounded off by a band with a wide repertoire, which includes old-style waltzes and show tunes as well as more modern music. But don't forget that your over-fifties guests are the original Beatles and Stones fans too! A more contemporary, informal wedding could be followed by a very modern band. However, there is no strict formula that you have to follow – ultimately it's all down to what you think will work best.

Do remember that a single performer accompanying themselves on the piano will be drowned out in a very big room, whereas a five-piece band will be overpowering and simply out of place in a small room.

Stand up for yourself and what you want, and don't agree to things you don't want just to keep the peace – you'll always regret it if you do.

Should we have a band or a DJ?

If you have the time and the money, have both. This can be the ideal way to cater to all tastes. A typical wedding band will play a wide range of songs from the sixties to the present day, ensuring your older guests will find something they like to dance to, and the DJ can finish off the celebrations by getting all the youngsters on the floor to dance to the latest chart hits. It also allows you to have a very specific type of band: jazz band, eighties band, Beatles tribute band, etc. You can then follow up with a DJ playing a broader range.

Before making a decision on this, check with the hotel about whether it's possible to get a bar extension. Some don't have this facility, which means you may not have enough time for both a band and a DJ.

Selecting a band or DJ

I'm starting to sound like a broken record here, but get any recommendations you can, and if you were particularly impressed by a band at your friend's wedding, get the name and contact details. Your hotel is also a great source of information – they usually keep lists of band names, and the wedding coordinator may even be able to tell you a little about some of them so you can decide if they're worth checking out.

When you meet the band's representative or speak to them on the phone, ask:

- ♥ What kind of music they play
- ♥ How many members are in the band
- ♥ What their fee is and how long they play for
- ♥ How many breaks they take and if they play CDs during these breaks.

You really need to see the band play live to decide if they're right for you. Generally the best way to do this is to go to see them play at another wedding. It's one thing to see them play in a pub, but the sound and their range of music can be very different at a wedding. Give the band a call and find out where they're playing next. If you know the venue well you may be able to do this surreptitiously, e.g. there may be a corridor or lobby near the reception room where you can sit and listen without interfering with the wedding party.

If you don't know the venue or feel you need to go into the reception room, make sure your contact in the band or their agent checks with the bride and groom if it's all right for you to pop in. Ask your contact where is the best place to stand – at the back of the room, near the bar etc. Don't turn up in your oldest jeans – you want to blend in with the wedding party, not stick out like a sore thumb! Don't try and talk with the band unless they're taking a break.

The bride and groom will more than likely have visited other weddings themselves to decide on a band, so as long as you're discreet they're unlikely to mind. In all likelihood they'll be too busy enjoying themselves to even notice.

Things to look out for:

♥ The quality of the singing and the music

♥ Is the band playing live, or using backing tracks?

♥ Is the lighting satisfactory – do they provide disco lights?

♥ Are they suitably dressed for the occasion?

♥ Is the band leader interacting well with the audience?

♥ Are guests out dancing or is the dance floor empty for long periods?

♥ Can you imagine your family and friends boogying down to this band?

You should need only about fifteen minutes to make an assessment. If you're unsure, by all means go to see them again – if you're still not sure, they're probably not the band for you and you should look elsewhere!

Once you've decided ...

Find out if a deposit is required, and how far in advance you need to meet the band to talk about a playlist.

Nearer to the Big Day ...

Meet the band or DJ and discuss what kind of music you want. For the DJ in particular, give them a list of the songs you really want to hear. If there are songs you particularly hate, give them a 'no way' list too.

Establish whether you want them to play requests from guests as the night goes on. Be prepared to allow flexibility in the playlist – a good DJ will be able to tell if something isn't working and should know what will get the crowd back on the dance floor.

Make sure the musicians have the contact details for the hotel, and if they haven't played there before, that they chat with the hotel about what time they can set up, access to power supply, and what time they should finish.

Your first dance

If you have a special song you want played for your first dance as husband and wife, see if the band can play it already or if they're willing to learn it. Otherwise you could have it played on CD – sometimes there's no one like the original. Arrange for someone to give the CD to the band in good time; this could be the groomsman's job. *See* Chapter 12 for first dance suggestions.

Alternatives

If you're tired of the normal wedding scene with a band and dancing, how about something else entirely? You could get some traditional musicians and organise a céilí, have a sing-song where everyone can join in, set up a casino, or have a table quiz where the questions all relate to the newly married couple.

CHAPTER EIGHT

The Beautiful Bride – creating the look

F inding your wedding dress is one of the most exciting, exhilarating, daunting, nerve-racking and wonderful parts of all the wedding preparations. It makes it all seem real at last. You try on a dress and when you look in the mirror you don't see the ordinary girl who walked into the shop; you see a bride. Best of all, once you've found your dress, your whole vision of the day becomes clear. It's so much easier to picture the ceremony, the reception, the flowers, the dancing, when you can imagine yourself at the centre of it all in your beautiful gown.

You may have been planning your wedding dress since you were a little girl. Perhaps you've made a mental note of the details of wedding dresses in your favourite romantic films.

You'll almost certainly have oohed and aahed over the ads in wedding magazines. So by now you probably have a very clear idea of what you want, or don't want. But can I sound a word of caution: please try not to be too firmly convinced. You really don't know what will suit you until you try it on. Try to put aside your preconceptions, go shopping with an open mind, and be willing to try on several different styles to find out what suits you best. The dress that looked stunning in the magazine might look very ordinary on you or just not suit your figure or skin tone. On the other hand, the dress that seems plain and uninteresting on the hanger might look stylish and elegant on you.

I speak from experience here: I had my mind firmly made up that I wanted a strapless dress with a fitted bodice, an A-line skirt, lots of sparkly diamanté detail, and it had to be white. I ended up getting an ivory, halter-neck, very plain dress which was long and flowy in simple Audrey Hepburn style (Can you tell I still love that dress almost as much as my husband? ... only joking, obviously). And most of the brides I talked to had similar stories.

When to shop

If you're planning on buying your dress from a specialist bridal boutique, you'll need to start shopping six to eight months before the wedding, as dresses can take quite a while to order in. The normal procedure is that you try on sample dresses in the shop, and when you've chosen one the shop will order a brand new one for you in your size, which will then be altered to fit you exactly.

Some shops sell the actual dresses that they have on display – they're the ones that ban you from wearing fake tan or make you wear white gloves when handling the dresses.

If you're happy to buy a dress 'off the peg', then you don't have to worry about looking so far in advance.

Leoné, Armagh

The very first dress I tried on when I got engaged was my mother's wedding dress. I wasn't seriously considering it, but something about it lingered in my mind. I did the rounds of the bridal boutiques but couldn't find what I was looking for anywhere. Eventually I realised why – I already had my mind made up about which was the dress for me. When I tried on my mother's dress again I realised it was perfect. It was a simple classic style that hadn't gone out of fashion and only needed minor alterations to fit me. On my wedding day not only did I get to wear a dress I loved, I had the link with my parents' wedding thirty years earlier.

What am I looking for?

Before you go shopping, think about your best and worst bits and how you want to highlight or camouflage them. The following are some hints on what may suit your size and shape.

If you are:
Short

♥ Wear heels, but only if you're comfortable in them. Dresses with vertical lines will give the illusion of height, and a train helps. An empire line dress will make your legs look longer. The simpler the style of the dress the better. Anything too heavy or overly decorated will emphasise your petite stature.

Tall

♥ Your biggest problem might be that everything looks good on you, as most dresses will suit tall brides. However, if you're self-conscious about your height, you can disguise it a little by choosing a dress with horizontal decoration at the shoulders or waist, or an off-the-shoulder style. You could also think about getting a two-piece dress, with the bodice and skirt in different colours. This will make you look smaller.

Large busted

♥ Choose a fitted waistline. Avoid heavy detailing on the bodice.

Small busted

♥ Go for a deep v-neck or invest in a padded bra.

Full figured

♥ Elongated waistline or empire line. A tightly-fitted bodice makes your waist look smaller and gives you an hourglass figure. Stay away from bulky or glossy fabrics.

Pear-shaped

♥ A princess line is very flattering, particularly if teamed with a detailed bodice to draw the eye upwards. A full skirt is good for hiding big hips and thighs.

An A-line skirt is flattering for all body shapes.

Going shopping

I read in numerous wedding magazines and books that I should bring the shoes and underwear I was planning to wear on the day when shopping for my dress. I'm afraid that's nonsense – how are you supposed to know before you've bought the dress whether you'll need shoes in white, ivory or any other colour, three-inch heels or ballet bumps, and so on? What's the point in shelling out a small fortune on a strapless bra only to find you need a backless one instead? Are you supposed to choose your shoes or underwear first and then buy a dress to match? I think not.

If you have a strapless bra, wear that. It doesn't matter if it's the wrong colour, it'll give you a better idea of what a strapless or spaghetti strap dress will look like than trying to squint so you can't see the bra straps tucked under your arms. Wear decent knickers and tights too – the shop assistant is going to be helping you in and out of the dress, so think twice about that red thong or those torn tights. Don't worry too much about shoes; most bridal boutiques will have shoes you can try on with the dresses.

If you have long hair that you intend to wear up on the day, put it in a similar style, or at least in a ponytail to give you a better idea of how necklines will look.

Look your best. Don't go shopping on the day you are coming down with the flu or suffering from a hangover. If you have no colour in your face or lips and your eyes lack definition, then not even the most expensive dress in the shop is going to look right. Remember how draining some of the wedding colours – white, ivory, pale cream – can be on the complexion.

Bring someone with you who'll give you an honest opinion, whether that's your mother, your bridesmaid or another friend.

The last thing you need is a gushy shop assistant telling you that every dress you try on is perfect, when you know very well that it's not. Someone who loves you and wants you to look your very best should always be trusted over someone just trying to make a sale.

Celebrity Style

Zoe Ball bought no less than four wedding dresses before she finally made up her mind which to wear – one was eventually worn by her sister-in-law, and another was made into a costume for her niece.

The truth about bridal shops

The staff in the shop where I bought my wedding dress could not have been nicer or more helpful and made the whole process an absolute pleasure, and I have no doubt that there are plenty more like them out there. Indeed many are not only skilled in finding the right dress for the right bride, but take a genuine joy in being part of your wedding, and their experience will be invaluable to you.

However, this book is all about helping you, the bride, so I would be falling down in my duty if I didn't prepare you for the fact that not this is not always the case. This may be a generalisation, and generalisations are always dangerous, but, based not only on my experiences but on those of dozens of brides I've talked to, bridal boutique sales assistants are possibly the most unhelpful, cynical and unenthusiastic profession you are likely to come across. Given that they make their living from the business of weddings, they are astonishingly oblivious to the fact that you are shopping for the most important outfit you'll ever own. Perhaps it's because they have, essentially, a captive market, or maybe that there isn't enough competition, or that brides-to-be are particualalry vulnerable; whatever the reason, it's not attractive.

One bride I know was openly laughed at in several shops when she told them she didn't want to spend more than €500 on her dress. A friend who is a size 16 was informed that they didn't stock any dresses for larger women and she would probably have to get one specially made. Another bride was sent away with the advice that it was far too early to look for her dress, only to be told when she went back at the time suggested that she had left it too late.

Molly, Kilkenny

I hadn't really started thinking about my dress, but I was out shopping on a fun girlie afternoon with two of my bridesmaids. As we passed a bridal shop I had an impulsive thought: let's go in for a quick look and a laugh. We had a look around and I picked out one that I thought was what I wanted. A very snotty (and skinny) girl told me I couldn't try it on and that in general they only stocked small-fitting dresses. However, they could order it for me in a larger size if I wanted to buy it, but I wouldn't get to try it on first. As if that was going to make me spend hundreds of euro! We were gutted. The two bridesmaids wanted to write to the manager and complain but what was the point?

I'm not trying to scare you, just to prepare you, and hopefully you will encounter only pleasant, helpful people. Remember that you are the customer. Be firm in what you want and don't want; you should never be made feel uncomfortable or embarrassed. And if you don't get the service you expect, then take your business elsewhere.

Plan of action

Make a list of bridal shops you want to visit, and call them to see if you need to make an appointment to try on dresses. Most insist that you do, which is really a good thing as it means you'll have the undivided attention of the sales assistant and won't have to share a cubicle with a bride you don't know (I've seen it happen). Plan your day carefully. Any more than three appointments in a row without a break for lunch or coffee, and your bridesmaid, or whoever you've brought with you, will be ready to kill you (or even worse, to tell you that any old dress is perfect just to get you out of there).

On your first appointment, try on at least five or six different styles of dress. You'll be amazed at how different the various shapes will look and feel on you. You may be able to rule out some styles straight away, but at least you've tried them on, and you'll have narrowed down your search.

Don't worry too much at first about details like embroidery, beading, lace and so on – these can be found on any style of dress. Concentrate instead on:

- ♥ The shape of the bodice – fitted, loose or two-piece
- ♥ The fullness of the skirt, from ballgown style to straight
- ♥ Sleeves: long, short, sleeveless, off the shoulder or strapless

The length

Necklines

Train – long, short or none at all.

Decide which features you like best and rule out any that don't suit you.

What Colour?

Married in White, you have chosen right,
Married in Blue, your love will always be true,
Married in Pearl, you will live in a whirl,
Married in Brown, you will live in town,
Married in Red, you will wish yourself dead,
Married in Yellow, ashamed of your fellow,
Married in Green, ashamed to be seen,
Married in Pink, your spirit will sink,
Married in Grey, you will go far away,
Married in Black, you will wish yourself back.

Queen Victoria is credited with starting the fashion for wearing white, as she wore white for her wedding to Prince Albert in 1840. Before her time, royal brides were dressed in silver.

A Little Bit of History

No matter how many times I told my husband that my dress was ivory, he kept referring to it as my beautiful white dress. I suspect he is not the only man who can't really tell the difference. You, on the other hand, will soon be an expert on every variation – white, offwhite, winter white, antique white, cream, ivory, champagne – and they've probably invented a few more shades by the time I've finished writing this sentence. But white and all its variants are certainly not the only options. White has declined in popularity in recent years, which I suspect has less to do with the scarcity of virgin brides than the fact that it can be very harsh on pale Irish skin. Ivory tends to suit a wider range of colouring.

Popular new choices are gold and silver, which still look very weddingy, or red, pink, lilac and blue, which are less so. Try dresses in several different colours and decide which works best with your skin tone. You can also mix and match: a gold/silver bodice and white skirt, etc. If you opt for a less traditional colour, be prepared for people to disapprove. Guests tend to be quite traditional about weddings and expect to see the bride in white. All that matters at the end of the day is that you love the dress and that your groom thinks you are a vision of loveliness.

Celebrity Style

Pat Kenny's wife Kathy eschewed traditional white and wore a green mini-skirt for their Paris wedding.

How big and fussy should I go?

Unless you make your living by starring in period dramas, you may never get another chance to wear an elaborate ballgown, so it's worth at least trying one on to see how you feel. If you don't like it or can't see yourself wearing something so heavy for a whole day, then forget it. You can still be a princess in a simpler dress. If you love it and feel comfortable in it, ignore any mutterings about 'meringues' and take the plunge.

How much should I spend?

Have a budget in mind before you go shopping. It's easy to get carried away, and the dress is one area where brides often end up spending way more than they had planned. That's fine if you can afford it or can make savings elsewhere. But if you really can't spend more than a certain amount, try not to look at dresses outside your price range so you won't be too disappointed.

Remember that expensive is not necessarily better. It doesn't matter whether your dress cost €20 in a Vincent de Paul shop or €5,000 in a designer boutique – if it makes you look and feel fantastic, then it's the one for you.

If you do fall in love with a dress that's outside your budget, see if you can make savings in another area. Perhaps you can borrow a friend's veil, tiara or even shoes, and put the money you had budgeted for them towards your dress. Otherwise, look back on the savings tips in chapter 3 and see if you can cut back even more! You may decide it's worth making sacrifices elsewhere so you don't have to walk down the aisle in your second favourite dress.

Lynn, Dublin

I got the idea for my dress at a friend's hen party. One of the girls was wearing a casual wrap-around skirt that you could wrap in either direction, so it was like two skirts in one. I thought it would be great to have a wedding dress with a skirt which could be reversed later in the evening. I love dancing so I liked the idea of blending in on the dance floor instead of being in a princess-type dress which people would have to dance around. I worked out the basic design I wanted – ballet-length, A-line, with a simple bow at the top of the bodice, and a bolero style jacket which would be lined in red. It took a lot of almost 'architectural' planning by the designer to work out exactly the best way to create a wrap-around skirt which wouldn't be too bulky or heavy. I had great fun on the night – the element of surprise was great when I appeared on the dance floor in a red skirt. My husband didn't have a clue what was going on at first! Plus it gave me a great excuse to invest in a pair of red party shoes for the disco.

How do I know I've found the dress for me?

The short answer is, you just do. Most brides fall in love with their dress the moment they try it on. Sometimes you can tell because you don't want to take the dress off; you'd be happy to parade up and down the shop admiring yourself until the staff actually have to throw you out.

If you don't get that feeling of absolute certainty, don't

worry, it doesn't necessarily mean you haven't found your perfect dress, you're probably just being a little more cautious. Maybe there are two or three dresses you could happily see yourself wearing. Don't just think about how it looks, think about how it makes you feel and whether you can imagine yourself wearing it all day and dancing in it all night. And if your mother bursts into tears the minute she sees you in it, that's an excellent sign.

Remember, the dress should make you look your best, not the other way around. When you walk down the aisle you want people to say 'doesn't she look beautiful?' not 'isn't her dress beautiful?' There's a subtle but vital difference.

If the search is getting too much for you, don't despair. Remember you had to kiss a lot of frogs to find your prince, and he was worth it. Your perfect dress is out there somewhere just waiting for you to find it.

If your problem is that you haven't seen any dress you truly like and you feel that you have looked at every dress within a hundred mile radius, maybe it's time to think about designing your own?

Designing your own dress

Even if you plan on designing your dress in conjunction with a reputable dressmaker, it's still a good idea to visit at least one shop to try on dresses. As I mentioned earlier, it can be quite a surprise to see what does and doesn't suit you. Note any features that you particularly like, and discuss these, plus your own original ideas, with the dressmaker.

You should also bring along sketches of your ideas, or pictures you've found on magazines or websites.

Allie, Dublin

I bought countless magazines to help choose a dress for the big day. However, once it came to trying them on I found it very hard to find a style to suit. On one particular shopping trip with my mum and sister, I tried on a dress and the sales assistant was explaining how she could adapt the dress to suit me. I could see my sister Carmel in the mirror taking it all in. Eventually, as I was getting out of the dress, Carmel whispered to me that she could make my dress. Carmel had made other dresses, so I wasn't in the least bit worried and I accepted straight away. Then it was off up to buy some material and a pattern. Carmel made me a beautiful dress and veil to match; I was so delighted because I got exactly what I wanted (and for a fraction of the price I would have paid in the shop!). My goddaughter even sewed sequins onto my veil and was thrilled to be part of it all too!

Alternatives

Hire your dress. Many bridal shops offer this service and you might be able to get your dream dress for a fraction of the cost of buying it. You're only going to wear it once, and if you're not inclined to be sentimental about such things, you're probably not going to want to keep your dress anyway.

Buy a dress secondhand. Check out buy and sell magazines, or the Buy and Sell section of websites such as www.weddingsonline.ie . Charity shops are worth checking out too – Oxfam shops in particular often have gorgeous designer dresses.

It's a new trend but one that is definitely gaining in popularity to try on your dress in a bridal shop and then order it over the internet, usually from America, at a lot less than the shop price. Some boutiques have cottoned on to this and cut the labels out of dresses so you don't know what you're trying on (which also makes it more difficult to shop around within Ireland).

There's no doubt that you're taking a risk by ordering over the internet – it could take a lot longer than you expected for the dress to be delivered. You may also be caught for customs duties on it, which would drastically reduce the savings you've made. But it's certainly worked out perfectly for several brides I talked to.

Wear a 'bridesmaid's' dress. Many bridesmaid styles are available in white, ivory and other bridal colours, and work out way cheaper than dresses designed for brides. I guarantee you; no one will know the difference.

Check out the eveningwear departments of high street shops. You could be lucky and find an evening dress that will be perfect for your wedding. A word of caution here – particularly if you are going for a non-white dress – you may run the risk of a guest turning up in the same outfit if it is a dressy wedding. Shop outside your local area, or pop across the border to Northern Ireland for something that will be less available.

A simple white summer dress would be ideal for a beach wedding, and you'll get to wear it again.

Watch out for sales in bridal shops. You can sometimes pick up a sample dress at a bargain price.

Celebrity Style

Some of the most copied celebrity wedding dresses were Posh Spice's ivory princess style dress with fitted corset, Caroline Corr's simple and elegant Vera Wang number, and her sister Sharon's halterneck dress with antique lace.

COMPLETING THE LOOK

Veils and headdresses

Whether or not to wear a veil is another common predicament for brides. I'm a big fan of veils – they really add to the glamour factor, and look particularly striking in photographs, but they don't work for everyone, and definitely don't go with every dress. Even if you're convinced you don't want one, it's worth trying one on to be sure; sometimes a veil can transform a plain dress into something really special. Veils come in a variety of lengths, from elbow length to the cathedral veils, which go all the way out to the end of your train. Try on a few with your dress, and see if it works.

A tiara can be teamed with a veil or worn on its own. You'll really feel like a princess when you try on a few gorgeous sparkly tiaras. It's also possible to get them specially made.

You could also consider a pretty jewelled comb, or the simple but classy option of flowers in your hair.

The Roman custom of the bride wearing a veil was to disguise the bride from the evil spirits and to keep her safe. Victorian brides wore a veil to symbolise modesty, respect and virginity.

A Little Bit of History

Shoes

Most bridal shops also stock shoes, which is very handy as you can try them on with your dress to make sure they suit. You can also get them from general shoe shops. Look out for sales – you can pick up real bargains, and who's going to know you're wearing last year's style?

Go shoe shopping in the evening; your feet swell during the day, so it's the best way to make sure you buy the size that will be comfortable for the whole day.

If you're buying a very high heeled or uncomfortable pair of shoes, why not buy a pair of white runners you can change into for the dancing – several companies are now doing special bridal trainers, with diamanté detail.

Don't forget to break your shoes in in the weeks before the wedding – *see* Chapter 14.

Underwear

Don't be deceived by the gorgeous lacy white bras and suspenders you see in the wedding magazines. If you're expecting to wear something like that you're likely to be sadly disappointed. Brides usually end up with underwear that is a lot more Bridget Jones than Samantha Jones. For one thing, many brides need the extra bit of help that those magical hold-you-in knickers provide, or the cleavage created by a Wonderbra. Remember that white underwear will often show through a white dress, so you may well have to go for flesh coloured (the underwear, not the dress ...). And then there's the fact that bridal fabrics tend to be quite sheer and smooth, so any lumpy bits of lace or design are going to be obvious. So choose your underwear for what will show the dress – and you – off to your best advantage, and keep the sexy stuff for your honeymoon.

If you need an extra bit of help to get the shape you want, you can get corsets specially made to fit you. They don't come cheap, but a friend of mine swears that hers was the best investment of the whole wedding budget. And support tights are a godsend.

Before you go shopping, get the advice of your bridal shop on what would work best with your dress. Bring a picture of your dress so you know how low it is in the back and so on. Make sure you buy your underwear before you have your dress fittings, and bring it with you so you can try everything on together.

Something Old, Something New...

A Victorian rhyme advises brides to wear:

Something Old,
Something New,
Something Borrowed,
Something Blue,
and a Silver Sixpence in her Shoe.

Something old represents a link with the bride's family and her old life.

Suggestion: a piece of jewellery belonging to your mother or grandmother, or which you yourself received as a present from a family member in the past.

Something new represents good fortune in the bride's new life.

Suggestion: any new item you're wearing – if not your dress, then your shoes, veil, tiara, or even underwear!

Something borrowed is ideally something that has been worn by a happy bride at her own wedding, but can be any item borrowed from a loved one. It's supposed to bring luck to the marriage.

Suggestion: any item borrowed from another bride, such as a veil, or a piece of jewellery borrowed from a family member.

Something blue comes from Biblical times, when blue represented faithfulness.

Suggestion: blue garter or a ribbon on your garter, blue ribbon or embroidery sewn on the inside of your dress or underwear, an ankle bracelet with blue stones, or paint your toenails blue!

Silver sixpence in her shoe represents wealth in the marriage, not just material wealth but the riches of joy and happiness together. This part of the rhyme is not as well known so brides often don't bother with it.

Suggestion: if you are keen on this but don't fancy walking around all day with something in your shoe, how about taping the coin to the outside arch or the inside of your high heel so it won't be noticeable?

Many brides choose to combine their 'something old' and 'something borrowed' by wearing a piece of family jewellery. One enterprising bride I know wore her mother's sapphire ring, thus sorting out her something old, borrowed and blue in one go.

BRIDESMAID DRESSES

I have heard rumours that some brides feel that the bridesmaids should look as awful as possible so that the bride looks fabulous in contrast. I'm sure you don't fit into that category, but if you're in any way tempted along those lines, remember:

- ♥ These people are your friends. You want them to feel good in what they're wearing and to enjoy the day (if not, why are you asking them to be bridesmaids?)
- ♥ Everyone knows that the bride picks the bridesmaid dresses, so they will think you have awful taste if you dress them in hideous shades or styles
- ♥ It's your wedding photos that are going to be ruined by acres of peach taffeta
- ♥ You are the bride. No matter what they wear, no one is going to look as radiant, happy and downright gorgeous as you.

So, having got that out of the way, how are you going to dress your bridesmaids so that they are happy and you achieve the look you want for the day?

Firstly, don't start looking at bridesmaid dresses until you've decided on your dress, as they should be of roughly similar styles. There's no point in dressing your bridesmaids in slinky little black numbers with a slit up the side if you're going to wear a big ballgown. And your dress is the most important, so theirs should fit in with yours, not the other way around.

Have a colour in mind before you go shopping. The colour of the bridesmaid's dress is usually the main colour of the wedding. Flowers, table decorations, favours etc will be tied in around it, so it's really the bride who should get to choose. However, if your bridesmaids really hate it, try to reach a compromise – they're the ones who are going to have to wear it.

If you want to tie the colour in to the season, think yellows and greens for spring, light blues, pinks and purples for summer, russet and orange for autumn, and reds and darker colours for winter.

Going shopping

If you have more than one bridesmaid, it's probably easier just to bring your chief bridesmaid with you on the initial trip to narrow it down. Once you've picked out a dress (or several dresses) that you both like, then you can call in the others. Bringing all the girls on the first trip will make it a lot more time-consuming and potentially contentious.

You may find it impossible to find one dress that suits their varying figures, colouring and taste. Traditionally, bridesmaids all wore the same dress; in fact, going back further in time, they wore the same dress as the bride, so as to confuse any evil spirits that might wish to harm her. Hopefully, you're not too concerned about that, and you also shouldn't feel obliged to dress all your bridesmaids the same. While it's still common to see bridesmaids in identical dresses, there's no reason why you have to conform.

There are a few different options you could consider to keep all the girls happy. The obvious one is the shape of the dress. Many dress manufacturers make up dresses that are in the same colour and fabric but of different design, particularly if they are two-piece dresses. One of your bridesmaids might wear a strapless dress and another a halterneck. If one is self-conscious about revealing too much flesh, she could get a dress with a higher neckline, or perhaps cap sleeves. If you have a pregnant bridesmaid, an empire line dress is probably the most comfortable and flattering style for her.

If it's colours that are the problem, consider getting the same dress in different colours. If you have two bridesmaids, two complimentary colours would be lovely, such as red and green for a Christmas wedding. For three or more, you could go for a variety of shades within the same colour band – pale lilac to purple, peach to flame, or sky blue, sapphire and navy.

Any of these options will still look very co-ordinated and stylish in your photos, and may mean you have a much happier group of bridesmaids to support you.

Don't restrict your search to bridal boutiques. There are evening or cocktail dresses that would be ideal for bridesmaids, and can be bought off the peg, saving time and money, and with the added bonus that the girls can wear them again if they wish. For more casual weddings, a trouser suit or co-ordinating skirt and top would make a refreshing alternative.

LOOKING GREAT ON YOUR WEDDING DAY

So you eat the odd (or maybe more) bar of chocolate; you sometimes go to bed without taking your make-up off; you went to the gym religiously for the first three weeks of the New Year and haven't used your membership since? That just proves you're human like the rest of us. But you'll never have better motivation than now to get yourself looking fabulous. Whether your wedding day is twelve months or three months down the line, start getting into those habits that we all swear by, but few adhere to.

Exercise

Walk. It's great for your circulation, for your legs, for giving you that feelgood factor that puts a sparkle in your eye. If you are not fit, don't be afraid to start small: park the car at the far end of the supermarket carpark, or an extra street away from where you work. Instead of hopping into the car for short distances, use your feet. Take the stairs rather than the lift at work, or the escalator in the mall. Go for longer walks at the weekend and drag your fiancé along for company. Swimming is also one of the best forms of exercise you can take as it uses a broad range of muscles. In those dark winter evenings, create your own exercise regime, which you can do while watching your favourite soap, or invest in an exercise bike or treadmill. Exercise will also help you beat stress.

Healthy eating

If you genuinely need to lose some weight, combine your exercise with a sensible eating plan. Avoid fad diets – they might help you lose weight quickly but it won't stay off. Dieticians always come back to the tried and tested formula of eating more fruit and vegetables and less fatty or sugary foods, and drinking tons of water – this makes your skin look better too.

Hair

Whatever kind of hair you have, keep it in good condition by having it trimmed regularly to get rid of split ends and dryness, and treat it to an intensive conditioner once a week. If you are happy with its current style, fine. If you want a new cut or colour, try it out at least a few months in advance. Don't attempt anything too dramatic with your hair just before the wedding. You want to look like yourself when you walk down that aisle – a more glamorous, beautiful version of your normal self of course, but not so different that your guests won't recognise you.

If you have short hair, don't feel you have to grow it for the wedding. It'll drive you mad and you'll probably decide to chop it off when you get back from honeymoon. Your hair is probably short because it suits you that way. A simple tiara or a hairpiece such as a bejewelled comb can look really lovely in short hair.

Teeth

Go to the dentist to make sure you get any necessary treatment out of the way well in advance of the wedding and honeymoon. While you're at it, get your teeth cleaned so you can flash those pearly whites with confidence for the camera. If they're really stained, you could consider having them whitened.

Beauty treatments

Now is the time to implement that beauty regime you've always been meaning to start but never quite got around to. Be strict about the 'cleanse, tone, moisturise' routine; it will become second nature to you after a week or two, and you will notice a difference. It's a good idea to have a facial to kick-start your new regime – it will deep cleanse those pores, get rid of dead skin and give you a great base on which to work. The beautician will also give you advice on taking care of your skin. Don't start the facials too close to your wedding – they often cause spots to appear, which is a good thing because it means your skin is cleansing itself of impurities, but not something you want to do just before the big day.

Get your make-up done at a beauty counter in one of the big department stores, and invest in some new products. For a real treat, have a make-up lesson. You'll learn invaluable tips, not just for your wedding but for the rest of your life. Experiment with several different products until you find a look you're happy with. If you're very particular you could even have someone take photos so you can see how it will look in your album.

Start exfoliating all over regularly and smothering yourself in body lotion after every bath or shower. Pay particular attention to dry areas like elbows and knees. Your arms will probably be on show in your dress, so make sure they're silky smooth.

If cellulite is a problem, try body-brushing before your shower to stimulate circulation. Some of the wonder creams available for cellulite busting really do work, but you have to use them regularly and they don't come cheap. Look out for tips in magazines and try the favourites.

Professional Make-up

If you want to get your make-up done professionally on your wedding day, book it early. Lots of make-up artists will come to your home to perform their miracles, which is very handy and leaves you with one less appointment to worry about on the morning of the wedding. If you're having yours done it's normal for you to pay for the bridesmaids to have theirs done too, and maybe your mum as well. Have a trial a few weeks in advance to make sure you're happy with the look.

Tanning

Lots of brides are of the view that a 'just back from a week on a golden beach' look is a must, probably because it does counterbalance the draining effect on some Irish skins of the white/cream wedding ensemble. It is, of course, a matter of personal preference, and you may not even be considering tanning for your wedding. But if you are, there is a huge range of options on the market now for fake tans: from the creams and mousses you apply yourself to the spray-on tanning offered by beauty salons. Whatever you decide on, be sure to have a trial run first. Exfoliate and moisturise regularly before having the treatment, paying particular attention to elbows, knees and hands. Listen to (or read!) the instructions about showering afterwards carefully. Note how long the tan lasts and whether it comes off on clothes or sheets.

If you are thinking of having sunbed sessions, you should really make yourself aware of all the medical warnings about the dangers of using sunbeds.

If you have trouble sleeping, try some of these tips: go for a walk an hour or two before bedtime, have a relaxing bath, put lavender drops on your pillow, have a mug of hot milk before you go to bed, or read a good book. A good night's sleep will make you look bright-eyed and bushy-tailed, and will help you feel a lot calmer.

CHAPTER NINE

Invitations

If you haven't already experienced this, then I hate to be the one to tell you, but the composition of the guest list is the part of the wedding planning most likely to cause rows between you and your fiancé, your parents, your future in-laws, and even your friends. Your father won't be able to understand why you don't want him to invite all his colleagues, and your mother-in-law will be outraged that you're not letting her invite her old school friend whom she hasn't seen in twenty years.

Lay down the ground rules as soon as you can so that everyone knows where they stand. You will already have decided on roughly the size and feel of your wedding, so you'll know whether you want to invite all and sundry, or keep it to those closest to you. Your venue may be a factor if it can hold only a limited number – registry offices in particular are normally quite restricted in terms of capacity. Make the limitations, and your wishes, clear to both families early on so they'll be prepared for the fact that they may have to go along with your game plan rather than their own.

Irish weddings were traditionally big family occasions that provided a chance for relatives who didn't see each other very often to talk about old times and find out what was new in each other's lives. While this is still true to a certain extent, couples are now more likely to regard the day as a celebration of their love and the start of their new life together, rather than as the joining of two families. This means that they would prefer to be surrounded by their own friends and people who care about them as a couple, not just people who know their parents.

If your parents are paying for the wedding, you'll have to allow them a bit more leeway on the guest list. However, this shouldn't mean that when you walk down the aisle you see more of their friends than of yours. It's still your day no matter who is paying for it.

If numbers are limited, give your parents a maximum number that they can invite, either including or excluding your aunts and uncles. The same goes for the groom's parents. Try to persuade them both that the guest list should be made up of people who know and care about you; their friends and neighbours who saw you grow up should be given priority over their old college buddies or cousins you don't know. Remember, there will be people on your fiancé's side who you've never met before, and vice versa, so there will already be plenty of new faces for you to get to know on the day, without inviting lots of people who neither of you have met.

As regards your own friends, you may find you don't have room for everyone and have to cut down on your list a bit. If you haven't seen someone in the last year, you probably won't see them in the next few years either, so think about crossing them

Lynne, Offaly

My parents gave us a very generous contribution to the wedding fund, but my fiancé's parents didn't want to know. So I couldn't believe it when he came home with a list of invitees that was longer than that of my parents and included all of their neighbours. There were over thirty people on the list, almost a third of the total guestlist of 100, and they 'couldn't possibly not ask any of them' because they had been to all of their weddings. After much discussion, we spoke to them and asked them to take people off. This didn't go down well at all and I had visions of my future mother-in-law taking out a contract on me. Eventually they realised that we just couldn't afford to bring everyone and agreed to reduce the number... phew! All we had to worry about then was where they would all sit!

off your list. Make exceptions, of course, for friends who live abroad. On the other hand, if you don't have a problem with numbers, a wedding invitation to someone you've lost touch with might be a way to rekindle your friendship.

It may help to ask yourself, if so-and-so was getting married, would you expect them to invite you? Also, if you don't know someone well enough to invite them over for dinner, then you don't need them to share in the most important day of your life.

Do we have to invite people 'plus guest'?

It's considered polite to add 'plus guest' to an invitation to a single guest so they can have the option of bringing someone if they dread the thought of going alone. However, this can increase numbers and costs quite significantly, as well as putting you in the situation of having a lot of strangers at your wedding. It may also put pressure on guests who would otherwise be happy to go alone.

Use your judgement. If your guest knows other people attending the wedding, then it's probably fine to ask them alone. And even if you do decide to give them the option, you may find they prefer to go alone rather than have to entertain someone who doesn't know the rest of the gang.

Celebrity Style

Madonna invited the girlfriends of male guests only if she had previously met them – supposedly to stop the Jack the Lad types among Guy's friends from using the wedding as a means of luring starstruck young females into their arms. Clever girl!

Do we have to invite our cousins?

No, you don't, whatever your mother or grandmother may be telling you. For some people it's simply not practical; there might be eighteen first cousins ranging in age from newborn babies to adults with spouses of their own whom you'd have to invite too. As a compromise, you could invite one representative from each family, usually the eldest, or else just invite cousins you were close to as you were growing up.

Do we have to invite our colleagues?

The people with whom you share your wedding day should be there because you care about them and not because of office politics. If you have a small group of co-workers who you get on well with, eat lunch with and socialise with, then by all means invite them. You could also consider inviting a larger group to the evening reception, if you're having one.

I found it impossible to choose between all my work friends, so I just invited one to the whole wedding, and then asked the entire company to the afters. It worked out really well. No one was offended (or if they were they didn't tell me) and I was thrilled when a large number came even though they had to make quite a long journey.

Good reasons to invite someone:

♥ You care about them and you want them to share your happiness

♥ Your day wouldn't feel complete without them

♥ You enjoy their company.

Bad reasons to invite someone:

♥ Your parents were invited to their daughter's wedding eight years ago

♥ You're inviting someone else who is a mutual friend and you don't want them to be annoyed that they're left out

♥ You think they'll buy you a nice present.

Will you be having children?

A question likely to be posed to you by nosy parkers, well meaning or otherwise, once you become newly weds – or even before. But in this case I'm referring to whether you want the little darlings as guests at your wedding. Some people think of weddings as family occasions that wouldn't be complete without gangs of children running everywhere and posing sweetly for photos. Others feel it's an adult occasion and that it's not fair to expect children to sit quietly during the ceremony or the meal – or, more to the point, that it's not fair on others to have them disrupting it.

Many couples limit the child guests to their nephews and nieces only; others decide not to allow even that. If you opt not to invite children (or just a special few), stick firmly to your decision. Don't be swayed by your friend moaning to you that she can't find a babysitter, or your aunt complaining that her daughters would be so disappointed not to see you in your wedding dress. If your guests really want to come, they will make alternative arrangements for the kids. Most parents will understand how you feel, and will even look forward to a day away on their own, where they don't have to miss the speeches to take little Johnny to the toilet, or leave the party early to put little Mary to bed.

How do we let people know?

If your invitation says 'To Kate and Steve', it means to Kate and Steve, and not Kate, Steve and baby Chloe. You shouldn't have to be any more explicit than that. If you're afraid that guests will bring children along uninvited (it has been known to happen), you could consider including a note on the information sheet with the invitation saying something like 'Unfortunately we are unable to accommodate children at the wedding'.

This could seem a little harsh, however, and it's probably best to spread the information by word of mouth instead. Parents will usually ring you or your mother to check, and there will always be some who think that their children should be exempt from the rule. Just be prepared to tell them firmly that you're not having children at the wedding. If you need an excuse, some of these should work:

- ♥ It's a formal, grown-up occasion
- ♥ Your venue has limited numbers
- ♥ There would just be too many children if you allowed all your guests to bring theirs
- ♥ You're keeping it to close relatives/flower girls/page boys only.

Step-families, family feuds and sworn enemies

In today's Ireland not everyone comes from the traditional nuclear family, and this may impact on your wedding plans. A friend of mine was best man at a rather unconventional wedding recently: the bride was his mother, the groom was an ex-priest, and the bridesmaid was his gay brother.

Yours might not be quite so unusual, but your guest list may include people who are separated or divorced, new partners, stepbrothers, half-sisters, in-laws and outlaws of every description. Equally, you might have uncles who fell out over the family farm, aunts who haven't spoken in ten years because of a row you don't quite understand or people who have had an acrimonious break-up but both remain friends with you. You might even have friends who are still on opposing sides in the Roy Keane debate, today's answer to the civil war. Maybe you're worried that if you invite them all your reception could be spoiled by bad feeling.

The only golden rule is that you should invite everyone you want to share in your day, notwithstanding any problems they may have with other invitees. They should all be adult enough to put aside their differences for one day. If you're having a big family wedding, there will probably be so many other guests that they don't even have to talk to each other. Your only headache should be in arranging the seating plan so that they're as far away from each other as possible.

I attended a friend's wedding where the guests included an RUC officer and an ex-IRA man. Recipe for disaster you might say, but no. The bride and groom made sure they were seated at different tables, and the two men simply ignored each other, not wanting to do or say anything that would take from the happy couple's day. If they could put aside their differences in the interests of a couple they both cared about, then so can your guests.

If one of your parents has a new partner, in almost all cases they should be invited, particularly if you get on well with them. You wouldn't want to be invited to a wedding without your partner, so your mum or dad will feel the same. This may be difficult for the other parent, especially if they're single, but if you explain your reasons to them they will probably be willing to make this sacrifice for you.

THE INVITATION

What should the invitation say?

At the risk of stating the obvious, the invitation should include your names, the date, time and place of the ceremony, reception details, and an RSVP address and date. You'd be surprised at how often printers catch an invitation before it goes to press with some vital detail missing. The following are are some sample wordings :

From the bride's parents:

David and Anne Pink

Request the pleasure of the company of

. . . .

at the marriage of their daughter

Mary

to

John Blue

On Saturday, 28ᵗʰ May, 2005

At two o'clock

At the Church of St John , Rathrock

And afterwards at a reception

in the Paradise Hotel.

RSVP by 30th April 2005

Parents' address

For a more formal wedding:
Mr and Mrs David Pink
Request the honour of the presence of
....
at the marriage of their daughter
Mary
to
Mr John Blue ...
Some women hate being called 'Mrs Husband's name' – if this sounds like your mum, then Mr David and Mrs Anne Pink is fine too.

From divorced parents who are co-hosting the wedding:
David Pink and Anne Pink
Request the pleasure of the company of
....
at the marriage of their daughter
Mary
to
John Blue ...
In this case, don't forget to specify who the RSVP should go to – it's up to yourselves to decide what makes sense.

From a remarried mother hosting the wedding with her new husband:
Mrs Anne and Mr Michael Green
Request the pleasure of the company of
....
at the marriage of her daughter
Mary Pink
to
John Blue ...

If you are paying for the wedding yourselves, you can still have the bride's parents as hosts on the invitation if that's what you want. Or, if you prefer, it can be from yourselves:

Mary Pink and John Blue

Request the pleasure of the company of

....

on the occasion of their marriage

on Saturday, 28th May, 2005 ...

Or you can include both sets of parents:

Mary Pink and John Blue

Together with their parents

Anne and David Pink

and

James and Patricia Blue

Request the pleasure of the company of

....

on the occasion of their marriage ...

Dont forget to include an RSVP date. Four weeks before the wedding date is about right – this means you can allow about a week for stragglers who only remember to buy a stamp on the RSVP date, and have plenty of time to chase those who still don't reply.

If you have a dress code such as black tie, that should be on the invitation too. A simple description ('Black Tie', 'Morning Wear' etc) can be placed at the bottom of the invitation, usually on the opposite side to the RSVP address.

Other information to include

Most wedding invitations now include an extra sheet of paper – or even a little booklet if you're feeling particularly adventurous – with all the details guests need to have an enjoyable and hassle-free day. The main things to cover are:

Directions to the church/venue and hotel, and a map if it's complicated. You could photocopy this from a town map, or just draw a rough one showing the main landmarks. This is often a good job to delegate to your dad; in my experience they love maps and figuring out routes. Before you finalise this, drive the route yourself to see that all the directions make sense, or better still, ask someone who doesn't know the area to do it.

Lists of accommodation in the area. Include a range of hotels, B&Bs and guesthouses to suit all budgets, and give approximate distances to your reception venue. You could also supply the number of the local tourist office, in case guests need any more information.

Any or all of the following would also be helpful:

♥ Names and numbers of local taxi companies

♥ Parking facilities at the church and hotel

♥ Names and numbers of local hairdressers and beauty salons

♥ Name and number of a local doctor, especially for families with small children

♥ Babysitting facilities, if the hotel provides them

♥ Location of ATMs close to the venue

♥ Availability of vegetarian and other special diet meals – sometimes the hotel will ask you for the numbers in advance, so if this is the case you should ask guests to indicate in their RSVPs if they need a special meal.

You may also want to send an RSVP card or your wedding gift list out with the invitations – more on this later in the chapter.

Choosing your invitations

This is another fun part of wedding planning! Wedding fairs are a good place to view the work of different designers. You should also check wedding magazines for ads, and have a look on the internet. When you find a supplier whose work you like, ask them to send you some samples.

The invitations are the first indicator guests will have of the style of your wedding, so choose carefully. Do you want them to say traditional/formal/classy/modern/relaxed/fun? It used to be that invitations were almost invariably on stiff white card, gilt-edged and with nice lettering, but the range and design of invitations has expanded enormously.

If you are getting your invitations done professionally, make sure the stationers supply you with a proof. Check the spellings of names and all details, and get someone else to check it too – you may have looked over it so often you miss something obvious. Order extras to allow for any errors you may make when writing them out.

Alternatives

If you have the time and are in any way artistic, think about making your own invitations. This could save you a lot of money, and make your invitations really unique. Try shops and specialist paper suppliers for materials. You could print the whole thing, or make the outsides by hand and just print the inserts.

If you don't have access to a printer but can create a design yourself, save it on a disk and bring it to a printing shop; this will still save you money compared to ordering invitations.

Creating your own invitations gives you a chance to have something that's really personal and reflects the interests of you and your groom. We had our First Communion photos on our invitations, which got a great reaction. A couple I know used an illustration of a type of knot used in climbing, a hobby they both enjoy, with the caption 'Tying the Knot'. Other friends got engaged on top of a Ferris wheel in Paris, and used a photo of it on all their wedding stationery.

If you have something you'd like to use but lack the artistic skills to put it together, some invitation suppliers will create a design for you based on your own ideas. This will obviously work out more expensive than choosing one of their existing designs.

For a smaller wedding, you could buy pre-printed invitations in a card shop, and just fill in all the details yourself.

When do we send them out?

Send the invitations between six and twelve weeks before the wedding. Less than six weeks gives guests very little time to respond. More than twelve and they may think it's too far away to make plans. Send them earlier for Christmas and overseas weddings.

It may be tempting to have an A and B list so that if any of your A list can't make it, you'll have room to invite a few more from the B list. However, most people realise that getting a late invitation means that they were not first choice, and you could cause offence. It probably wouldn't work anyway – you're more likely to get early RSVPs from people who are coming than from those who aren't.

By the way, you *should* send invitations to members of the bridal party, to your brothers and sisters, and the groom's parents (yours too if the invitations are from yourselves). This may seem a bit silly when they know all the details already, but they will love to have them as souvenirs.

Create a spreadsheet with a list of all your guests – it will make it easy to keep track of RSVPs, and you can add a column for presents to help you write your thank-you cards. Or use a site like www.ezweddingplanner.com. For the less technologically-minded, a pen and paper with ruled columns will work just fine.

Invitations to those who can't come

Close friends and family will appreciate receiving an invitation even if you know they can't come – at least they'll feel you wanted them to be part of your day. However, don't fall into the trap of issuing invitations out of politeness to extra guests who you feel safe in inviting because you're sure they won't come. There are always shocks with the RSVPs. People you thought were dead certs to accept suddenly can't make it, and guests you invited to keep someone else happy, but were sure would refuse, accept your invitation with alacrity.

Evening invitations

Most Irish weddings include an evening reception, or 'afters', where guests not invited to the wedding join the party at around eight or nine for dancing and the evening buffet.

Wording for the evening invitations:
David and Anne Pink
Request the pleasure of the company of
……………………
at an evening reception
to celebrate the marriage of their daughter
Mary
To
John Blue
on Saturday, 28th May, 2005
at eight o'clock
at the Paradise Hotel

It's also quite common to put the names of the bride and groom as hosts on the evening invitations, even if the day invitations are from the bride's parents.

You don't need to send evening invitations as early as day ones: three or four weeks before the wedding is fine. But do send them earlier for any guests who have to travel.

RSVPs are not usually required for evening invitations, unless you need to give the hotel exact numbers.

RSVPs

Even in this modern age when a lot of wedding etiquette has been thrown out of the window, it's still the height of bad manners not to send an RSVP to a wedding invitation in good time. Nevertheless, a surprising number of guests fail to do so, causing a real headache for brides in the last few weeks before their wedding, when they have dozens of other things they need or want to be doing besides chasing recalcitrant guests. My husband thought we should just ignore non-respondents and assume they weren't coming, but I was haunted by the thought of people turning up on the day and the hotel having run out of food.

Some couples choose to include RSVP cards with the invitation so that guests have even less excuse for not responding. You could get these printed along with your invitations, or print them yourself in simple postcard style with your address on the back, so an envelope isn't required.

In the US these are usually stamped, but that's certainly not expected here. In fact, pre-printed RSVP cards are still fairly rare, and it's nice to have a collection of the different ones that guests have bought if you're planning to keep a wedding scrapbook or keepsake box.

You could also consider including an e-mail address to which people can send their RSVPs, or set up a special one for your wedding – this is very handy for guests and may make your life a lot easier.

Chasing difficult guests

The RSVP date has come and gone, and you still haven't heard from twenty guests. You really shouldn't have to ring them all yourself, so delegate. Get your mum to call any non-respondents from your family, your fiancé's mother to call any from hers, and your bridesmaid to call your friends. Ask them to explain to the guests that you need to let the venue know final numbers and to do up your seating plan.

Save-the-date cards

Save-the-date cards are another American concept that have found their way across the Atlantic. They are simple little cards, which are sent out in advance of the invitations, asking guests to keep the date free. They're a good idea if you're getting married in the summer when you might be competing with summer holidays or other weddings, at Christmas time, or on a weekday when guests will need to book time off work.

You could order them from the company that is doing your invitations, or make them yourself; they don't have to be too fancy. For summer or early autumn weddings, you could send them out with your Christmas cards to save on postage. Also, people will be getting their new diaries at that point and can enter the date straight away.

Alternatively, send e-mails to those with internet access at least six months beforehand, asking them to keep the date free.

GIFT LIST

Unless you're like Rachel from 'Friends', wedding presents are not going to be the most important thing on your mind when planning your day, but they're a nice bonus all the same. Your guests are going to want to buy you something to mark the day. A gift list is a great idea for both the couple getting married and their guests. For you, it means you get lots of useful presents that are right for you or your home, instead of the clichéd five toasters and monogrammed towels that clash with your bathroom suite. For your guests, it makes life a lot easier, as they can just contact your chosen shop(s) and choose something off a list, safe in the knowledge that you're going to like it.

What you put on your wedding gift list depends on your individual circumstances. Some couples will need practically everything, while if you are lucky enough to have a house or apartment already, chances are that you will also have furnishings, bed linens, etc, so many of the usual gifts aren't needed. But there may be many things that you haven't got around to buying or would like to replace. Your wedding list should set you up for married life, so now is the time to assemble the dream dinner service/glassware suite for all those dinner parties you're going to host as a married couple. Too expensive to buy in one purchase, your guests can buy them as individual items. Make a wish list (try not to fight over it) and bring it with you when you go to the department stores. Do give guests plenty of choices. They won't all have deep pockets or may not fancy giving you a single plate from a very expensive collection, so try to include lots of items in the more reasonable range too.

Your gift list should include things that you need but also things that you just want but wouldn't buy for yourself. This is the time to indulge your fantasies. It's like being a child again and making a list for Santa, if not more fun. In the US, they have gift lists for engagement parties, bachelorette (hen) parties, bridal showers and even – as 'Sex and the City' fans will know – baby showers. On this side of the Atlantic, we only get to do it once, so make the most of it!

Alternatives

Think about having a different kind of gift list; it could include vouchers for a weekend away, horse-riding lessons, a meal in a nice restaurant, whatever takes your fancy. Check out www.giftvouchershop.ie for ideas. Also, some travel agents will set up an account for you where guests can contribute towards the cost of your honeymoon, so perhaps a four-star hotel in the Caribbean isn't beyond your means after all.

If you or your groom are the outdoors type or have a particular hobby or sport, have an alternative list at a shop that caters for your interests.

Are there any craftspeople or tradesmen among your guests? The promise of a fitted wardrobe, built in hob, shower installation etc is a gift worth a lot of money nowadays.

You could also ask guests to make a contribution to charity instead of buying you a present.

Celebrity Style

Catherine Zeta-Jones and Michael Douglas asked their guests to make a donation to a charity they set up in the name of their son, Dylan, in lieu of wedding gifts.

Set up the gift list before you send out the invitations. Once guests receive their invitations, they'll start thinking about buying you a present. However, don't do it too early, as some of the items you choose could go out of stock or be discontinued. Three to four months before the wedding is about right.

Do we mention the gift list in the invitations?

In the UK it's quite common to include with the invitations a little card from the shop where you have your list or to mention it on the information sheet. In Ireland you'll find that while some people think that's fine and that it makes things very convenient for them, others are inclined to look askance at this and to wonder whether you're inviting them because you want their company or you're looking for a present. To avoid ruffling feathers, it might be best not to include it with the invitations, and just to let people know by word of mouth. Make sure both mothers and members of the bridal party know where you have your list, as guests will be just as likely to ask them as to approach you directly.

Most wedding guests today are happy to buy from a list and will ask if there is one. The people who don't ask are the people who don't want to be told.

Maria, Longford

We were aware that even though we were doing a list, not everybody would be happy or comfortable being told to use it. It can also send a message that you wouldn't be as grateful for something else, which isn't the case.

We decided to leave it out of the invitations, and we found that the vast majority of guests either asked us or asked our mothers. Our list was cleared in no time. In fact, we had to add to it! Guests were delighted that we had a list; at least they knew they were getting us something we wanted and would use.

In the end we got everything we wanted and no one was offended. And it was nice to get a few surprise presents as well.

If you're not having a list but are hoping that people will give you cash instead of presents, I'm afraid there's really no polite way to say this in the invitations. Some people advocate including a cute little rhyme to ask for cash, but think about this – even if you wouldn't be offended to receive this as a guest, would someone of your parents' generation? Really, the best way is by word of mouth; if people ask your mother what you'd like, ask her to say, 'Oh, Sarah and John have everything they need for the house, but they're saving to build an extension/go on an extended holiday/buy some new furniture after the wedding' – and guests should take the hint.

CHAPTER TEN

Before and After: From hens to honeymoons

THE HEN PARTY

If you've been to hen parties before, you probably looked forward to them with glee – a wild night out for you and the girls and much amusement to be had at the expense of the unfortunate bride-to-be.

Suddenly it's your turn, and the idea may not be quite so appealing. You're the one who's going to have to persuade a strange man to give you his boxers, while wearing outsize L plates and a bit of a net curtain and penis-shaped zog-a-bongs on your head. Not quite the picture of glamour and sophistication you like to imagine yourself.

The typical Irish hen party is either a night of going out

somewhere local to eat, drink, dance, club, wear silly accessories and do daft things, or going away somewhere for the weekend to eat, drink, dance, club, wear silly accessories and do daft things.

The weekend away option is becoming increasingly popular, whether it's to another part of Ireland or somewhere in Europe – Edinburgh and Barcelona being particular favourites. Some brides even make a real holiday of it and go away to the sun for a week, thus acquiring the desired-for tan.

That's all very well if you all have plenty of money, but consider your friends' budgets before deciding to do anything very expensive. Weddings are a costly time for guests too. Your friends will be paying for a new outfit, shoes, accessories, hairdo, make-up, beauty treatments, and possibly accommodation and travel expenses also. A weekend away may be putting them under extra pressure, especially if your friends include students or those with new mortgages or babies. A night out in your own town can be just as much fun and enable more people to join in. And at least you'll be able to nurse that horrendous hangover in the comfort of your own home instead of having to face up to the return journey.

If the thought of a typical hen night really does fill you with dread, why not do something completely different.

Slumber party

Send your fiancé away for the night and invite the girls over. Rent a few videos – wedding-themed ones are ideal, such as *Four Weddings and a Funeral*, *Father of the Bride*, *Muriel's Wedding* or *My Big Fat Greek Wedding* – but possibly not *Runaway Bride*.

Get into your pyjamas and tuck into wine, crisps and dips (or hot chocolate, marshmallows and ice cream for a real pyjama party feel). Paint each other's nails and try out new make-up. Armed with an empty wine bottle, have a game of Truth or Dare (be warned – this can be dangerous!)

And when your fiancé gets home, be sure to tell him you all had a pillow fight in your underwear.

Theme party

Another party at home idea – or, better still, in your bridesmaid's home so she can do the cleaning up. Have a sixties/seventies/eighties night, make people dress up accordingly, and dance all night to old favourites. Or tie it in to your favourite film: *Grease*, *The Rocky Horror Picture Show*, *The Sound of Music*, *Romeo and Juliet*, *The Witches of Eastwick*.

Adventure day

Why should the boys get all the fun? Book a slot at a go-karting centre and race your friends around the track. Book an indoor soccer court and have five-a-side matches. Go paintballing. Head off on an adventure weekend of hiking and camping.

Pampering sessions

Book yourselves in for a day – or weekend – of pampering at a health spa. Get a facial, body wrap, massage, sauna, jacuzzi, manicure, pedicure. And it will be such innocent fun you can even invite your mother-in-law.

Ladies Day at the Races

Book your own private section at one of Ireland's many racecourses. Dress up to the nines and have a 'best hat' competition. Have a brilliant day betting on the horses, and enjoying a few drinks in the company of your best friends. Finish off the day with dinner at a nice restaurant. A less expensive alternative would be a night at the greyhound track.

Cruising, Irish-style

Rent a boat on the Shannon or Lough Erne for the weekend. Moor at different towns for food, drinks and a chance to sample the local scenery.

More party-at-home ideas

- ♥ A cocktail party. Get everyone to bring different ingredients – fruit, juices, paper umbrellas, stirrers and as many kinds of alcohol as you can think of – and try out as many recipes as you can find
- ♥ A poker night – all you need is a pack of cards and poker chips; matchsticks will do
- ♥ A lingerie party – the hen's answer to Tupperware
- ♥ Have a make-up artist come to your home and give you all a make-up lesson. You'll pick up some great tips if you are doing your own wedding make-up. This works best with small numbers, and is another event you could easily invite the mothers to
- ♥ Have a spooky night, with a séance or a fortuneteller to read your Tarot cards.

Who organises the hen party?

Traditionally, it's the chief bridesmaid's responsibility to organise the hen party, but maybe the task would be better suited to one of your other bridesmaids – or perhaps you don't trust any of them and would rather do it yourself!

If you're letting your bridesmaid organise it, be sure to tell her what you do and don't want. If you really dread the idea of being made to dress up, say so – it's your party and you shouldn't be made to feel uncomfortable. Of course, if you did anything awful to your friends when they had their hen parties, you can expect them to take their revenge!

Make sure she has the phone numbers or e-mail addresses of everyone you want to invite, then leave it up to her to do all the planning and ringing around.

It's a good idea to set a date for the hen party a few months in advance. This is especially important if you're going away or have friends coming from out of town. Even if neither of these applies, it's still a good idea to take time to pick a date that suits everyone, and make them put it in their diaries to avoid disappointment later.

Have the hen party at least two weeks before the wedding. You'll need to keep the weekend before the wedding free for things like dress fittings, last-minute shopping for your honeymoon, and making final arrangements with suppliers. Plus it might be an idea to have plenty of time to recover from any alcohol-related catastrophes.

Should I invite my mother and mother-in-law?

They probably won't expect an invitation, so invite them only if you think they'd enjoy the kind of night you have in mind, they won't cramp your style, and it's easy for them to get to the party venue. Many mothers would hate the thought of drinking games and stumbling around looking for a taxi at four in the morning, but maybe yours would love it!

Lots of brides are now choosing to have several hen parties, partly to deal with this kind of dilemma. You could have a wild night out with all your friends, then a sophisticated, grown-up evening with female relatives, and maybe even a special night just for you and your bridesmaids. Multiple hen parties can also solve the problem of finding a date, venue and budget to suit everyone – and you get to enjoy them all!

Caitriona, Cork

I had what's called a kitchen party, a tradition in Cork. All female relations from my family and Paul's came, as well as friends. It was a brilliant night. Everybody brought a wrapped present for the kitchen and then I was blindfolded and had to guess what the present was and whom it was from. These parties were originally for when a bride would be marrying straight from her parents' home and wouldn't have anything for her kitchen. It's progressed a bit since then; I got some great presents and also some funny ones like inflatable boobs, face massager, as well as things I mightn't have bought for myself, such as a garlic press and a banana hanger. It was a mad night!

THE STAG NIGHT

Is it just me, or are stag parties becoming tamer as hens become wilder? Maybe it's just that you rarely see gangs of men stumbling about Temple Bar on a Saturday night wearing tacky costumes or matching headgear (and thank goodness for that, too).

You're bound to be a bit worried about what your fiancé's friends have in store for him on his stag night. My biggest fear was the classic shaved eyebrow trick – I had visions of walking down the aisle to a groom with one real eyebrow and one painted on. They take a long time to grow back, you know. I had the idea of asking one sensible, reliable friend, who could be trusted not to get completely hammered and would never give in to peer pressure, to look after him on the night – then realised that he possessed no such friends.

In the end, I needn't have worried. The night started off with such wild antics as the whole gang betting on the result of the Eurovision Song Contest, which was followed by outrageous tricks like spiking beers with milk and sugar, and the worst thing that happened to my husband-to-be was that he was put into a shopping trolley and pushed down a hill, which, when you think about it, is bad enough, but could have been a whole lot worse.

The best way of saving yourself a night of worry is to organise the hen and stag for the same night – that way you'll be too preoccupied about what terrible things your own friends have in store for you to think about shaved eyebrows, stolen clothes, and being tied to a lamppost (unless your friends are as bad as his).

THE REHEARSAL

The rehearsal is normally held in the week before the wedding. If members of the bridal party are coming from out of town, it could take place the night before. Arrange this with the celebrant a few weeks in advance.

It's usually only the bride and groom, bridesmaids, the best man and groomsmen who attend, but if you want to include your parents or people doing readings, you can. The rehearsal can really help to make you feel more relaxed on the day.

The rehearsal dinner

Please don't look at this heading with a sinking heart and think 'oh no, not another thing I have to organise'. The rehearsal dinner, normally held in a restaurant the night before the wedding, is an American tradition. It's certainly not expected in Ireland, but it is gaining popularity here, although it's not always known by such a formal name. It's a nice way for the two sets of parents to get to know each other a bit better, and adds to the sense of excitement and anticipation. From a practical point of view, it means no one has to cook on the night before the wedding.

If you decide to have a rehearsal dinner, you might want to invite your parents, members of the bridal party and their partners, other siblings, and any special out-of-town guests who may be at a loose end, but try to keep numbers to less than twenty.

In America the rehearsal dinner normally includes speeches, but that's not usually done here. If the bride's parents are paying for the wedding, the groom's should offer to pay for the meal; otherwise, let everyone pay for themselves.

THE DAY AFTER THE WEDDING

Lots of couples are now making their weddings a weekend-long affair by planning something fun for the day after the wedding. It doesn't have to be anything formal – in fact, after the formalities of the wedding day it's better that it isn't – but you may as well make the most of having all your friends and family around you.

You could have a party in your home or your parents' home – a barbecue in summer, a mulled wine party in winter, or a brunch at any time of year. Better still, if you have any money left over after the wedding expenses, get caterers in to do the food to save you a lot of work.

You could also arrange a gathering in a pub, and get them to provide cocktail sausages and sandwiches, which shouldn't be too expensive.

Other options could be a game of golf, a day at the beach, a countryside picnic, or a meal in a restaurant for close family and friends.

Deirdre, Dublin

My husband has supported Bohemians since he was tiny. They were playing in the last match of the season the day after our wedding, and being a very kind wife I agreed we would both go. We were congratulated over the tannoy at the stadium, which was weird but really cool. The team won the match, thereby winning the league for the first time in twenty-three years. My husband assured me that at least he would never forget his wedding anniversary; he would know it was the day before this famous victory!

There's a huge potential for anti-climax the day after the wedding, so having something planned is a great way to counteract that. And hearing people tell you how fabulous your wedding was will really send you off on honeymoon with a happy glow.

THE HONEYMOON

Whole books could be, and indeed are, devoted to the honeymoon alone, so I'm not going to even begin to look at the range of options you can choose. Just a few pieces of advice:

Don't go away on honeymoon the day after the wedding. You'll want to spend a bit of time with people you don't get to see very often and bask in the compliments about how well the day went. Above all, you will be exhausted, and travelling is the last thing you'll feel like doing.

If time allows, think about having a few days away somewhere in Ireland before jetting off to your honeymoon destination. This will allow you to unwind properly and just have a very relaxing time, without feeling you're wasting some of your precious 'exploring' time in a place you might never visit again.

If you are going off straight away, don't organise anything too energetic for the first few days of your honeymoon. If you're having a very action-packed trip, at least plan to have a few lazy days at the start. Don't underestimate how tired you'll be after all the hard work leading up to the day and the emotional impact of the wedding, which can really take its toll on you.

Don't have unrealistic expectations of your honeymoon. If you've been away together on holiday before, the honeymoon is really not that different. Yes, there's an extra romantic factor, and a wonderful newly wed glow, but there's also the anti-climax of the wedding being over to contend with. Just plan to enjoy it as you do any holiday, and if you're all loved up that's an added bonus.

Book any plane tickets in your maiden name, even if you intend to change your name after the wedding. It's possible, though not straightforward, to get a passport in your married name before the wedding if you have a letter from the celebrant, but it will only be a temporary one which you'll have to replace very soon afterwards. And since the passport office is now charging you the full price of a new passport to change your name on your passport, it's really not worth the expense or the grief. *See* Chapter 15.

CHAPTER ELEVEN

Getting Married Abroad

ill having a wedding at home mean that you have to invite a huge number of people, whether that's an enormous Irish family or a wide circle of friends and colleagues? Do you hate the thought of being the centre of attention at such a huge gathering, and the stress and hard work that the organisation entails? Then an overseas wedding has obvious appeal. You can keep numbers to a minimum, inviting only those who you really want to share in your day, or simply have it all to yourselves, if that's what you prefer.

Getting married abroad is the ideal solution for a romantic day without the fuss. You're more or less guaranteed good weather if you choose the right climate. You can have a beautiful and stunning setting – and one that's unique among your peers, which is very important if you've been to dozens of local weddings.

Susan, Mayo

When we first got engaged we planned to have a traditional big white wedding at home. But within a few months, rows had erupted over the guest list, and costs were spiralling out of control. After finding me in tears over the bridesmaid dresses, my fiancé suggested we pack it all in and get married in Rome. It was the best thing we could have done – we had a lovely, intimate wedding with the people we care most about, and managed to have our romantic day at a fraction of what the original plans would have cost.

Is an overseas wedding right for you?

Planning a wedding is a stressful experience; didn't someone once say that it's up there with death, divorce and moving house? At some point in their plans almost every couple will think, 'I wish we could just go off somewhere and get married'. But before you take the plunge, ask yourselves if you're sure it's what you really want, and that you won't regret not having a more traditional wedding.

Are you prepared to accept the fact that you probably won't get to see your wedding location in person before the big day? Are you willing to trust someone else to make the arrangements for you?

What about your friends and family? Will your parents be upset that they won't get to celebrate your marriage with everyone they wanted to invite? If you intend to invite family and friends to travel with you, will they be able to afford it? If you're going alone, will you be lonely for them, and will it be an anti-climax after you've taken your vows and no one's throwing a party?

Take all these issues into consideration before making up your mind that getting married abroad is the best option for you. If you're sure, be prepared to defend your decision until people get used to the idea. Then take the time to rejoice in the fact that you get to have a wonderfully romantic wedding with a lot less to worry about.

Where's it to be?

A historic European city or a glitzy American one, a remote and unspoiled beach, or surrounded by green countryside – let your imagination run wild. Maybe there is a particular location that means a lot to you as a couple, or somewhere you've always dreamed of going. If you simply have a vision of a sandy beach or a beautiful rural setting, get lots of brochures from travel agents and browse to your hearts' content.

Bear in mind that while more exotic locations may be tempting, European destinations will make it much easier for family and friends to join you, if that's what you want. Rome is a perennial favourite with Irish couples, and I also know of couples who have recently married in Cyprus, Turkey and Switzerland. You don't have to limit yourself to destinations where weddings are organised by travel agents, but if you decide to go it alone you'll have to deal with all the paperwork and formalities yourselves, and some countries make this more difficult than others.

Celebrity Style

Caroline Corr got married in a beautiful old stone church in a medieval village high in the mountains of Majorca. The setting was made all the more romantic when a power failure meant the ceremony took place by candlelight.

Sorting out the formalities

The legality of your marriage is governed firstly by the country where the marriage takes place, and the formalities can be quite different from those in Ireland. For example, in most other countries a church ceremony does not have the legal recognition it has in Ireland. In some countries, couples wishing to marry in church must also have a separate civil ceremony to make the marriage legally binding.

The couple whose wedding was dubbed 'Ireland's royal wedding', Taoiseach's daughter Georgina Ahern and Westlife singer Nicky Byrne, discovered that their church wedding in France would not be legally recognised, and had to arrange a civil ceremony in the Wicklow registry office a few days beforehand. They had a wedding co-ordinator to sort it all out for them, which I suspect you don't, so make sure you thoroughly check all the legal requirements in good time. If you do need to have a civil ceremony as well as the church one, you can choose whether to have this abroad on the same day, or at home beforehand. A civil wedding in Ireland will be easier to arrange, and there are residency requirements for civil wedding abroad which you may not be able to fulfill.

If you're booking your wedding through a travel agent, they will tell you what paperwork you need to complete and help you with all the necessary arrangements. If you're organising the wedding yourselves, the best place to go to find out what formalities must be observed is the embassy or consulate of the country where you plan to marry. For religious weddings, contact your local clergy who should be able to put you in touch with someone in the relevant area.

Eligibility to marry

As well as meeting the legal requirements of the country where the marriage is to take place, you also have to have the capacity to marry under Irish law, as outlined in Chapter 5. For example, it's possible for a sixteen-year-old to get married in Scotland, but if you are an Irish citizen, the marriage won't be recognised here because you must be eighteen or over to marry.

In some countries you must provide a Certificate of Freedom to marry; this is sometimes called a 'Certificate de Coutume' or 'Certificate of Nulla Osta'. To apply for this, contact:

Consular Section
Department of Foreign Affairs
72-76 St Stephen's Green,
Dublin 2.
Tel: 01-4082568
E-mail: marriageabroad@iveagh.gov.ie

If you are living abroad, contact your nearest Irish embassy.

If your marriage is taking place in Rome, the Department

will send the certificate directly to the Irish embassy in Rome, and they then forward it to the relevant district. For most other countries however, the certificate will be sent directly to you.

You will also need to bring your birth certificates and valid ten-year passports with you when you travel. Be aware that some of the countries you may be planning to visit require you to carry a passport that is still in date for a set number of weeks/months *after you leave* that country. If, for example, you intend to travel on 6 June for a two-week honeymoon, and your passport expires on, say, 31 July, you could be turned back on arrival, if indeed you have not already been prevented from travelling by the airline staff at your home airport, who don't make the rules, but could be fined for allowing you to travel. Your travel agent should be able to advise you on this, and if you are still in any doubt, contact the embassy or consulate of your destination country for information.

Registration

When Irish citizens marry abroad, the marriage is registered in the country in which it takes place. The General Register Office in Ireland does not register foreign marriages, and it's not part of their duties to offer advice in this area.

Your foreign marriage certificate is normally acceptable in Ireland as proof of marriage, however if it's in a foreign language you will be asked to provide an official translation.

SOME FAVOURITE LOCATIONS FOR OVERSEAS WEDDINGS

Rome – Church wedding

Rome has been the foreign location of choice for Irish couples for years. Steeped in history and romance, the city makes the perfect setting for a wedding, and it's convenient enough to invite family and friends to share in your day. For many Irish Catholic couples the location has a special religious significance, as couples who marry there get to meet and be blessed by the Pope during his weekly public audience.

Because of the long history of Irish couples marrying in Rome, you'll find the formalities are relatively straightforward in comparison to newer destinations. If you don't want to deal with a travel agent, your parish priest should be able to put you in touch with the local authorities and make the initial arrangements for you.

The church normally used by Irish couples is San Silvestro, or the Irish College for group ceremonies, when several couples get married at once. A group ceremony is usually chosen if the couple are travelling alone or with a very small group.

If you decide to hire a travel agent, they will be able to sort out all the arrangements for you: a hotel wedding reception, photographer, flowers, and even booking a hairdresser for the bride. You might decide to dispense with a reception altogether, especially if there are only a small number of you travelling, and just pick a charming little restaurant where you can enjoy a relaxed meal, preferably in a piazza where you can watch the world go by. With larger groups, you could consider booking a whole restaurant for the wedding party.

Heavy traffic and chaotic driving make transport around Rome a bit problematic, so try to choose a venue for the meal that's within walking distance of the church.

If you decide to make all the arrangements yourselves, research locations over the internet and in guide books. Once you find a suitable hotel, whether it's for a reception or just for the two of you to stay, the staff should be able to advise you of other local services such as hairdressers or florists.

Take full advantage of the location to pose for your photos. The Trevi Fountain makes the perfect backdrop – no wonder so many brides and grooms are to be seen posing in front of it – and you can even enjoy a *gelato* from one of the nearby ice cream parlours.

One of the best things about getting married in Rome is the wealth of honeymoon destinations near at hand. The Amalfi coast, especially Sorrento and Positano, is a popular combination with Rome for a two-centre holiday, and the picturesque countryside of Tuscany is only a short train journey away, or you could hop on a plane to Sicily.

Beach weddings

Fancy taking your vows at sunset with the sand between your toes and strolling along the water's edge hand in hand with your brand new husband, wearing a floaty white dress or just a bikini?

The islands of the Caribbean, especially St Lucia and Barbados, and of the Indian Ocean, such as Mauritius and the Seychelles, make idyllic settings for weddings. A travel agent is definitely your best bet for making the arrangements; many will organise everything you need to combine your wedding with a dream honeymoon. Some will even offer the wedding part for free as part of the package.

Be sure to find out how many weddings the location caters for every day. Many couples have been disappointed to find that instead of exchanging their vows on a deserted beach or on a verandah overlooking the ocean where they feel they are the only two people in the world, they are in a queue of several other couples doing the same thing. Also, be clear on what the package includes. Beach weddings are by their nature very simple, but you may want flowers, champagne, photographs, music, and food – so check whether these are available and whether they cost extra.

Jen, Dublin

We decided to get married in Turkey because we got engaged there, but also because of its excellent climate, beautiful coastline and friendly inhabitants. Our wedding ceremony was held in Bodrum Castle, one of the world's best-preserved medieval monuments, with panoramic views of the bay. We had the civil ceremony first, which was conducted in Turkish and English, followed by the blessing where we got to exchange our rings. Afterwards we went to a beautiful restaurant, which we had found on the web. The view was amazing, it was very private and the food was to die for. The resident guitar player provided us with music, which set a perfect romantic ambience throughout the evening. When we got back to the hotel, the beachside bar had been decorated for us and everyone was holding sparklers to light up our arrival. All in all we had a fabulous wedding, which was romantic, exotic and unique.

Las Vegas

How about being married by 'Elvis' himself in the Little White Chapel? Las Vegas is the perfect wedding location for the minimum of fuss (and some would say taste, but who cares, it's your wedding) and as Britney's experience proved, you don't have to give any formal notice, or even be sober, to tie the knot there. Just turn up – you can even have a drive-through wedding – and spend the money you've saved from not having to buy bridesmaid dresses and flowers on the slot machines.

DON'T FORGET

If you are marrying abroad you will have a few more things to think about:

♥ Invitations. If you are inviting family and friends make sure to give them plenty of advance notice so they can make travel arrangements

♥ Transporting your dress. Make sure you plan how you're going to bring your dress. You can't exactly roll it in a ball and stuff it in your suitcase (well, maybe on the way home). Some airlines will let you bring it on as hand luggage – others are stricter and will insist it is checked in. Ring your airline in plenty of time to see if they can make any special arrangements for you

♥ Rings and essentials. Make sure your wedding rings and anything else you can't do without go in your carry-on luggage.

CHAPTER TWELVE

Celebrating in style – the Reception

WINING AND DINING

Guests are normally welcomed to the reception with a drink. Traditionally this would have been champagne, but you could also have sparkling wine, which is much cheaper. For summer weddings, Buck's Fizz, Pimms cocktails or a fruit punch would be a lovely alternative, and for winter you could have mulled wine or hot port. Tea and coffee are usually served also. You don't have to provide food at this stage, but you might want to consider having strawberries with your champagne, biscuits with tea and coffee, or crisps and nachos, if there is a long interval until the main meal is served.

For ideas for music for the reception, *see* Chapter 7.

The menu

It's better to keep the menu fairly simple when you're catering for a large number of guests; it's the easiest way to ensure that everyone will be able to enjoy the meal. Something that looks good in a magazine or sounds impressive on the menu is not necessarily what guests will enjoy. It's probably best to resist the temptation to be wildly original in your choice of menu, especially if your guest list includes fussy teenagers or people who just don't like unusual food. Guests will be hungry after a long day; often people don't eat lunch before wedding ceremonies, so the last food they had may have been breakfast. They're not going to want anything too fancy, just good food that's well prepared and nicely presented.

Many hotels will charge you an exorbitant price for offering a choice of meals, so do so only if the food is one of your main priorities.

Celebrity Style

At the wedding of Georgina Ahern and Nicky Byrne, guests were treated to Dublin Bay prawns and smoked salmon, roast veal, and ratatouille pie with parmesan cheese, followed by an unusual dessert of orange-flavoured Dacquise, crème brûlée and liquorice ice cream.

Don't forget to make provision for those with special dietary needs, such as vegetarians, diabetics and coeliacs. Check with the hotel as to what they can provide.

Depending on your venue, you may have the option of a sit-down meal with waiter service, a buffet where guests help themselves and then return to their tables, or a more informal buffet without set places or even seats.

If the hotel doesn't offer menu tastings, go for a meal in their restaurant to see what the standard is like.

Wine

Wine etiquette has shifted considerably in recent years, so the rule of red wine with red meat, and white with fish and poultry is no longer strictly adhered to. Unless you are very well acquainted with the preference of your guests, it is best to ask the hotel's advice on the proportion of red to white that is likely to be consumed.

Some hotels include wine in the set price, but most charge for it by the bottle. It can be quite expensive, and you are limited to the hotel's choice of wine – often one with which you will not be familiar. You may decide to supply the wine yourselves, giving you a much broader range to choose from, and the possibility of saving some money into the bargain. Off licences may give you a discount for buying in bulk. Look out too for special offers from chains like Tesco or Superquinn; you could pick up a real bargain. Get e-mailed information on their latest offers or wine sales so you never have to miss out on the deal of the month.

You could even take the ferry to France and buy your wine there. Even with your travel costs, you'll save a small fortune compared to what you'd pay in Ireland. Or consider popping across the border to Northern Ireland where alcohol prices are considerably cheaper. We saved at least 20% by buying our wine in Derry, and the champagne was half the price.

However, before you go down the DIY route, check out the corkage you will have to pay (corkage is a charge applied by hotels and restaurants, per bottle, to serve wine that is brought in by the customer). If it is high it can wipe out any savings you will have made by buying yourself.

In terms of the quantity to buy, remember that, as a rough rule of thumb, you will get five glasses from the normal size bottle of wine.

Clarify with the hotel whether they should put the bottles of wine on the tables, or have waiters go around topping up people's glasses. The latter option will appear a little fancier, but in fact will save you money, as you can dictate how often they should go around.

The toast

Champagne is traditional for the toast, and gives a lovely celebratory effect. You could also consider sparkling wines or Cavas. A good brand can be just as delicious and unless your guests are connoisseurs, they're not going to know the difference.

Some couples choose to let guests order a drink from the bar for the toast. This can work out a lot more expensive; you would be surprised how many people will order a double vodka just because it is free, and there is also the possibility of being overcharged on the final bill. On the other hand, it means that everyone gets the drink they want.

How much drink are we expected to pay for?

Wine with the meal is pretty much a must. I have heard of couples who decided not to serve wine and just to let guests buy their own drinks from the bar, but I can't help thinking that the guests were probably very unimpressed and moaned about it to everyone they know.

You can get away with not serving either champagne or a round from the bar for the toast if there's still wine on the tables; make sure the waiting staff fill up people's glasses so they have something to toast you with.

Unless you're the child of a millionaire, don't even think about putting money behind the bar. Free bars are the norm at American weddings, but it's just as well that's not the case here; unfortunately it's one of our less attractive national characteristics that it's compulsory to drink a free bar dry.

The evening reception

If you're having guests who are just attending the afters, an evening buffet is a must. It doesn't have to be anything too fancy: sandwiches, cocktail sausages, chicken nuggets, mini pizzas and crisps are the usual fare, accompanied by tea and coffee. You could also consider serving your cake at this point. People are often too full to eat any after the meal and will appreciate it more later on.

CREATING A THEME FOR YOUR RECEPTION

You could theme your wedding to the time of year:

In spring, use pastels and yellows, decorate tables with daffodils and tulips or those pretty, painted eggs that are on sale around Easter. Give guests packets of seeds or little potted plants as favours.

For an autumn look, decorate tables with apples, pumpkins and berries.

Create a winter wonderland with an all-white theme. Decorate the tables with white feathers and snowflake confetti and hang clear fairy lights around the room.

For Valentine's Day fill the room with hearts: scatter paper or metallic hearts over the tables, hang them overhead, give 'love heart' sweets to the guests.

Christmas can be very colourful in reds and greens. Decorate tables with holly, ivy and crackers, hang mistletoe overhead, name the tables after Christmassy things, give guests Christmas tree decorations as favours.

Or you could be really different:

Have a fairytale wedding. Hold the ceremony in a castle, arrive in a horse and carriage, wear a princess style dress, name the tables after fairytale characters, and have a cake shaped like the witch's cottage from Hansel and Gretel.

Celebrity Style

Madonna and Guy Ritchie kept their reception in line with local Scottish tradition: a main course of haggis was followed by an evening of céilí dancing. However, unlike most Scottish weddings, the guests were all in bed by midnight, probably worn out after a week of celebrations that included baby Rocco's christening and Guy's stag party in a local pub.

DRESS CODES

Black tie weddings are extremely stylish and may be the only chance you ever get to see your family and friends dressed up to the nines, and they make for stunning photos. However, bear in mind that a lot of guests find them a nuisance, and many people resent being told what to wear. It's mainly the men who will be affected by the 'black tie' rule, as women don't tend to wear anything very different from what they would normally wear to a wedding. For those who own their own tuxedos it will be an opportunity to get out their finery, but not too many men fit into this category, so you are putting them to extra expense, and they may feel uncomfortable in black tie anyway.

If you do decide to go for black tie, contact a local suit hire company to see if you can arrange a bulk deal, so that guests can rent tuxes at a discount. Include this information with the invitations.

CHILDREN AT WEDDING RECEPTIONS

Receptions can be long and dull for children, and you don't want them getting bored, becoming fretful and noisy and ruining the night for their parents and other guests. Keep them entertained by having something special in their place when they sit down – perhaps a little toy (not something noisy) or a colouring book and crayons. Make sure there are child-friendly meals available. Not all parents want their children to eat sausages and chips, so see if the hotel will do half portions of the main meal instead.

If you have a lot of children attending, consider putting on some special entertainment for them: a clown, magician or just a room where they can go to watch videos.

It's usually best to sit children with their parents so they can keep an eye on them, but if you do decide to have a special children's table, make sure you have one or two responsible adults supervising. Don't sit teenagers with younger children unless you've specifically asked them to keep an eye on them. They'll resent being unpaid babysitters, or worse, feel aggrieved that you regard them as children too.

THE SEATING PLAN

Drawing up the seating plan is one of the major headaches of the planning process, particularly since you won't be able to finalise it until you have all your RSVPs, and there are always stragglers.

Do we have to have a seating plan?

You might feel that a seating plan is more trouble than it's worth, or that you don't want to dictate to guests where they should sit, but if you have any more than fifty guests, it's difficult to do without one. It really does make things run more smoothly: you won't have people rushing around trying to find room for everyone in their gang, friends or even couples being separated, or your elderly grandmother being forced to sit next to your mad friends from work.

You know your guests best, and you'll be pretty sure about whom they'd like to sit beside. While you'll be hoping to introduce people from different parts of your lives to each other, guests generally prefer to sit with people they know, so try to achieve a good balance. If you really don't like the idea of a seating plan, you could, as a compromise, just assign guests to particular tables, but not to particular seats.

If you are having a seating plan, make sure to have it displayed at the entrance to the room. Better still, copy it and have one on either side of the doorway, to prevent crowds gathering and blocking the way.

To save time when drawing up the seating plan, write everyone's name on a post-it, which you can stick on to a big chart and move about as necessary until you've finalised the plan. It will save you endless amounts of scribbling.

The top table

This can be a nightmare! The traditional top table is one long table with people seated at one side only; this gives the rest of the guests a good view for the speeches.

Normally the people who sit at the top table are: the bride and groom, the chief bridesmaid and best man, bridesmaids, groomsmen, the bride's parents, the groom's parents, and the celebrant, if he or she attends. The bride and groom are in the centre, and you can arrange the others any way you wish.

Traditionally, the bride's mother sat with the groom's father, and the bride's father with the groom's mother, but if the two sets of parents don't know each other well then it's fine to just put each parent with their own partner.

Where parents are separated or divorced, either with or without new partners, difficulties can arise. You could consider having no parents at the top table – just have your bridesmaids, best man and groomsmen, and have one or two tables close by for all the parents, which could also include siblings.

1: Bride
2: Groom
3: Chief Bridesmaid
4: Best Man
5: Bridesmaid
6: Groomsman
7: Groom's father
8: Bride's mother
9: Groom's mother
10: Bride's father

If you still want your parents at the top table, then it's fine to have your parents and not their new partners, though it's probably best not to sit them together – mix them up with your partner's parents instead. They are at the top table in their capacity as your parents, not as a couple, so the new partner shouldn't feel aggrieved. After all, the best man's wife or the bridesmaid's boyfriend doesn't sit at the top table. However, if you decide to do this, try to make sure the new partner is sitting with people he or she knows, perhaps with their own children, or if this doesn't apply, maybe you should consider inviting them to bring their own guest for the day.

If the new partner has played a big part in your life, and it will not create any friction, why not have them at the top table too. There's nothing to say you can't have three or four parental figures there to support you!

If family arrangements become too complicated, or you just hate the thought of being the centre of attention, you can dispense with a top table altogether. Seat yourselves at one of the ordinary tables with the bridal party, but make sure it's in a good position if you're planning to have speeches after the meal.

TABLE DECORATIONS

If your wedding is in a hotel, they will usually provide some kind of table decorations, such as flowers or candles, so it's worth finding out what they do before committing your time and money to devising your own.

If money's no object, get your florist to make up special centrepiece arrangements in your chosen wedding colours.

Other ideas:

- Bowls with floating candles
- Bottles of bubbles, party poppers or streamers on the table create a party atmosphere
- Decorate with lots of balloons
- Scatter rose petals, metallic confetti or feathers over the tables
- String fairy lights along the top table and have a bowl of small fairy lights on each table.

Favours

Favours are optional; you don't need to have them, but they are a nice touch. Decide whether you want to give something really unusual, something guests can enjoy on the day, or something to remember the day by.

In parts of Europe, sugared almonds are the traditional gift to guests from the bride and groom – usually five almonds tied up in tulle, representing health, wealth, long life, happiness and fertility.

In the days before smoking bans, a very popular table gift at Irish weddings was a white box of matches, with the bride and groom's names printed in gold, along with the words, A Perfect Match. How times have changed!

Chocolates are now a popular choice in Ireland, and many of the companies who do handmade chocolates will supply them in a little box printed with your names and the wedding date. This is the perfect option if you don't want to go to too much trouble.

Lots of brides choose to make, or at least assemble, their own favours, to give it the personal touch. If you want to do this, consider the following options:

- Little tulle nets filled with chocolates, sweets or sugared almonds, tied with ribbon in the colour of the bridesmaid dresses
- Bookmarks printed with a romantic verse, your name and the date of the wedding; these are very cheap to make if you have access to a printer, and look lovely.

Julie, Meath

As favours, I bought plain shot glasses and painted each one with a guest's name. It didn't cost much but took absolutely hours! The effect was worth it, though – it looked so great to see them on every table, and our guests thought they were really unusual.

If you have a little more to spend, how about:

- The single of your first dance song on CD
- Flower seeds or bulbs, which guests can plant and remember your wedding by

♥Little candles

♥Miniature guest soaps or bottles of bubble bath

♥Mini bottles of spirits

You can use the favours as placecards, writing the guest's name on the favour itself or attaching a name tag with ribbon. Otherwise you could put them in a pile in the centre of the table.

SPEECHES

When do we have the speeches?

Speeches are normally after the meal, and are followed by toasts and the serving of the cake. This marks the end of the formal part of the day. Some couples decide to have the speeches before the meal; if speakers are nervous, it means they can relax and enjoy the meal. However, this can create difficulties for the hotel, especially if you're having a hot starter, and it's always difficult to estimate how long the speeches will take. It can also be a nuisance for starving guests who may not have eaten all day, and they may not give you their undivided attention.

Who speaks?

Traditionally, the speakers were the father of the bride, the best man and the groom, but more and more brides are choosing to make speeches, and sometimes bridesmaids too. You might also want the groom's father to make a speech on behalf of his family.

Try to keep the speeches short and sweet – no more than half an hour in total – to make sure you hold people's attention.

The best man acts as chair, unless there's a toastmaster. The usual order is: bride's father, groom, best man, groom's father, then any other speakers. You don't have to stick to this, though, just do whatever feels right.

The father of the bride:

Thanks everyone for coming, especially those who have travelled long distances

Praises his daughter and tells little anecdotes about her childhood or teenage years (NOT embarrassing ones. I had to get my mother to act as censor)

Welcomes the groom into the family

Finishes with advice to the groom, based on his experience of marriage (if happy) and his knowledge of his daughter.

If your father is no longer with you, your mother could speak instead, or perhaps your brother.

The groom:

Thanks the bride's father for his kind words

Thanks the bride's parents for the reception, if appropriate

Says a few nice words about his new wife

Thanks those who have made an important contribution to the wedding, such as the celebrant

Raises a toast to the bridesmaids.

The best man:

Replies on behalf of the bridesmaids

Congratulates the newly-wedded couple

Tells a funny story or two about the groom – but nothing too risqué

Speaks about the bride and groom's relationship and

how pleased he is that his brother/friend has found such a wonderful wife

💜 Reads some of the more interesting cards or faxes from absent friends

💜 Closes with a toast to the bride and groom.

If the bride speaks, she:

💜 Thanks the groom's parents for making her feel welcome in their family

💜 Thanks her own parents for everything they have done for her

💜 Thanks her bridesmaids

💜 Says a few nice words about her husband.

I chose to speak after my dad so I could get my retaliation in first, so to speak, but many brides opt to speak last, perhaps introducing their speech with something like, 'I'll start married life as I mean to go on, by having the last word'.

If the bridesmaid speaks, she:

💜 Says a few words about how happy the groom has made her sister/friend

💜 Thanks the groom for his toast (if she is speaking before the best man).

My father-in-law was most impressed that my sister and I both spoke (Women speaking at weddings! What next? was the general attitude). As far as I was concerned, after doing most of the planning, I wanted to say my piece on the day, and I felt my sister was just as important to the wedding as the best man.

One thing to remember if you're having more than the usual number of speeches is that everyone should compensate a little by making their speeches slightly shorter. People have short attention spans, so four or five different speeches might work better than three long ones, but not if they go on for twice as long.

Máirín, Wicklow

As part of my speech I read out a marriage contract that my husband had to sign. It included issues such as custody of the television remote control; the amount of time he can spend watching Sky Sports; decibel levels for his music; number of Friday nights he can spend with my brother in support of Bray Wanderers. It ended with an undertaking to end any disagreement we may ever have with, 'Yes dear, you're right, I'll buy that for you now.'

Christine, Dublin

Rather unconventionally, I started my speech with a toast to 'Barry from Limerick', the guy I was supposed to be going on a date with the night I met my husband. It got everyone laughing – especially my husband!

THE ENTERTAINMENT

Make sure you've talked to the band or DJ about the type of playlist you expect – *see* Chapter 7. There are also a few other things you'll need to consider.

The first dance

For most newly weds this is one of the most romantic parts of the day, when you first take to the floor together as husband and wife.

If you're nervous about it, why not have a few dance lessons? This might be the only time you'll be able to persuade your partner to come along with you. You could even surprise your guests and dance a tango!

If you have a song that's 'your song', choose that for your first dance, as long as it's romantic and easy to dance to. If the band don't know it, see if they're willing to learn it (you'll need to let them know in plenty of time); otherwise just have it played on CD.

You may not have a special song, so here are some suggestions:

The Way You Look Tonight (Frank Sinatra)
You're the One (Shane McGowan/Máire Brennan)
In My Life (the Beatles)
Grow Old Along with Me (Mary Chapin Carpenter)
It Had to be You (Frank Sinatra)
At Last (Etta James)
The Wonder of You (Elvis Presley)
Just the Way you Are (Billy Joel)
(Everything I do) I Do It for You (Bryan Adams)
True Love (Bing Crosby & Grace Kelly)
For more suggestions see www.simplyweddings.com.

The first dance is usually followed by a dance for all the members of the bridal party. The best man dances with the chief bridesmaid, and groomsmen with other bridesmaids. Your parents can join in this dance too, maybe the groom's father could ask the bride's mother to dance, and vice versa.

If you don't want to be in the spotlight, get the rest of the bridal party to join in after the first verse. Alternatively, you could forget about the first dance altogether. Get the band leader to call everyone onto the floor right from the start.

After these dances it's a free-for-all and all the guests can join in.

Aoife, Wicklow

After our first dance, I had arranged a special dance for me and my dad, as a surprise for him. It wasn't anything mushy, just a song he used to sing to me when I was tiny. My dad was stunned and then proceeded to tell me I couldn't dance for toffee ... well, I believe that I inherited that from him!

Tossing the bouquet and removing the garter

These traditions normally happen at some point during the evening entertainment. Get the band leader to call all the single female guests onto the floor, and toss your bouquet over your shoulder. Tradition claims that the one who catches it will be the next to get married. If you don't want to give away your bouquet, get the florist to make a special mini one for throwing, or throw the bridesmaid's bouquet instead.

Removing the garter is similar to the bouquet toss, but with less taste. The bride sits on a chair on the dance floor; the groom removes her garter (possibly with his teeth) and throws hated that idea. OK, so you've got the rest of your lives together, whereas you might not see some of your guests again for ages, but to me the whole point of the day was us being together. So we made sure we got to spend lots of time with each other: dancing together, alone or in a gang of our friends, introducing each other to relatives, and even sneaking away to the bridal suite for a quiet drink and a chance to open some of our cards.

One of the most common regrets which brides and grooms have is that they didn't get to talk to everyone on the wedding day. Don't feel bad about this. If you have a big, or even medium, wedding, it's virtually impossible to talk to everyone. Guests will still enjoy the day as part of the group, and between you and the two sets of parents and siblings, it's unlikely anyone will be ignored completely by the immediate families.

At one wedding we attended, the groom came up to speak to us at the drinks reception, then said, 'Wait a minute, I can't talk to you, you're not old!' and abruptly walked off. He was trying to get all the polite chats with 'old people' out of the way early on so he could relax and spend time with his friends later. I'm not advocating such a clearly ageist approach to socialising with your guests, but it's certainly one way to make sure you have at least a quick word with all the important people.

Another friend says he really regrets not getting more time to dance to his favourite songs. He had painstakingly put together a list of must-play songs and didn't get to dance to any of them because he was moving from guest to guest to talk. So try to do a bit of everything, while remembering you're only one person, and as I mentioned earlier, the minute hand is simply whizzing around the clock.

CHAPTER THIRTEEN

Here comes the Groom

THE TRUTH ABOUT MEN AND WEDDINGS

By Aidan Fitzmaurice

[Note from the author: The views expressed in this chapter are those of my husband and I take no responsibility for the consequences if you let your intended read them!]

It's probably not a good thing to admit. A bit like saying that you don't like puppies or that you're a racist. But the reality is that most men have little, if any, interest in the finer details of the wedding. They're interested in getting married.

Now, I know this is not what women want to hear, as they dash from dress shop to hairdressers to florists to tanning shop, stress levels and credit card bills going up, weight dropping off and hair falling out. But, really the only thing that is surprising is that women are surprised by this information. Men and women are different, though if you didn't know that by now, well, you shouldn't really be getting married!

For many girls, their wedding day is something they have dreamed about since they were little. Boys didn't. We dreamed about different things: scoring the winning point in the Munster final, saving a penalty for Ireland at the World Cup finals, playing lead guitar at Madison Square Gardens. Our bodies and our brains are different.

So it's the same with a wedding. For most brides, it's all the small stuff that adds up to a whole lot. Which is why they buy wedding magazines, books (like this one), go to bridal fairs, spend days, weeks, months, looking for that unique wedding dress. They obsess for hours over which centrepiece to get, scour entire continents looking for those oh-so-perfect shoes.

And the groom? If you're anything like this former groom, you will worry very little about the small stuff, but listen to an awful lot of talk in the weeks and months building up to the day, absorbing around 30% of the information into a brain which is already full of thought about important matters such as the best centre forward partnership/Six Nations try/'Father Ted' line/debut single/guitar riff/Beatles album/Irish novel in history.

Once you've got a nice suit, a comfy pair of black shoes and a smart enough haircut, then you're all set for the big day, and you should have plenty of time to sneak in a nerve-setting gin and tonic (but just the one, mind) an hour before the kick-off, while your bride-to-be is in a panic over whether the hair really works.

She will worry for months about the mass booklet: shape, paper size and colour, fonts, binding. *He* will probably end up calling it 'the programme'. *She* will have endless shopping trips to find the perfect little handbag for the bridesmaids. *He* won't even remember what colour their dresses were.

Being honest, I don't think I was all that concerned about the flowers in the church, the colour of the wedding car, whether the bride's shoes were too strappy. My mind was occupied with higher matters, my main concern being whether the DJ would play 'She Bangs The Drums', 'Baggy Trousers', 'Here Comes Your Man' and 'Alternative Ulster', and would I get away with more than two tracks from The Clash?

That's not to say I wasn't bothered about the wedding. Men are *bothered*, or they wouldn't be getting married in the first place. But if the average groom is anything like me, he's just happy that he's marrying the best and most beautiful woman the world, whether she's putting her hair up or wearing a woolly hat. So if you are expecting your groom to enthuse about the perfume of the flowers, the shape of the wedding cake, or notice that the table centrepiece is made of Waterford glass, then all I can say is, I'm sorry; you're on a loser there.

For the average male, all he wants is to get married to the woman of his dreams, in front of all the people the couple care about, to have a nice meal and a bit of a dance afterwards. Whether the reception takes place on the sunniest, warmest day of the year in the most expensive, most exclusive hotel in the country in front of 300 people looking and smelling better than ever before in their lives, downing the best food and champagne in the country – or whether you go for a small meal in a modest restaurant after a low-key service at the Registry Office, it won't matter to 88% of men. They are just happy to be married.

Of course, there are some grooms who let the side down by taking an active interest in all aspects of the big day, and if that's you, well then congratulations, you've already made a good start to married life.

But, to all the brides-to-be reading this who are finding it difficult to deal with their (normal) man's lack of interest in the whole wedding build up, don't worry. A lack of interest in the finer details of the day doesn't mean a lack of interest in getting married.

A word of advice to the men: handling this whole pre-wedding situation can be tricky. Just like opening one of those new TetraPack cartons, it could leave you in a hell of a mess. But there are ways of dealing with it.

Don't ignore all the details of the wedding, and don't leave everything to her or her mother – it's not a good start to married life. Take some interest, and share the workload. You could look after the non-girly stuff, like the wedding car, music, honeymoon and booze.

You can also play a vital supporting role by making sure that your bride, who will become more stressed as the day draws near, has less to worry about in relation to stuff outside the wedding world. In my case, I may have contributed very little in terms of ideas, organisation or even listening to the wedding arrangements. (And I will have that on my permanent record, taken down and to be used as evidence against me in the future, no doubt.)

But on the other hand, I also made sure that in the weeks and months building up to the big day, my fiancée hardly had to cook a meal, wash or iron clothes, or do the grocery shopping.

I admit that I did very little to help with the details of the wedding, but when she came home from a stressful day of shopping or meeting wedding-related people, there was always a dinner on the table, food in the fridge and clean clothes for work for her next day.

That won't work for everyone, especially if you're not living together before the wedding, but you can still try and share the burden. If you're not that bothered about the wedding cake, then let her look after that, but make sure there's something nice and a fresh pot of coffee for her at home when she's finished a hard day of wedding business. Let her obsess about the headdress, you make sure there's orange juice in the fridge and that 'Coronation Street' is taped.

For the brides-to-be, don't expect your future husband to be as interested in the wedding as you are. Let him in on the plans and tell him broadly what you want, but don't have every conversation for the last six months of your engagement taken up by wedding talk. He'll get bored, you'll get annoyed because he's not listening, and next thing you know you're in the middle of a big row when you should be looking forward to the happiest day of your lives.

Don't force him to do things that he doesn't want to do. If he hates dancing, don't push him to take ballroom dancing lessons. If he hates formal wear, don't make him wear a penguin suit. Don't insist on having a video made of the day if he can't stand the idea.

And don't forget that your wedding is only one day. You have a lifetime of marriage to take care of when the dancing stops. Try and think about what happens when you are actually married, not just who sits where on the big day. Have at least one night a week where wedding talk is banned. Try and talk about how your lives will change afterwards. There's not much point in having all that nice Denby crockery (a present from your aunt Dymphna) if you haven't thought about who's going to wash it after use.

Marriage is an honourable estate, as they say in the Protestant wedding service. It's also meant to be an enjoyable one. So enjoy it, don't overkill it.

A FEW TIPS FOR GROOMS ...

Proposal

Do it your way. Why go down on bended knee in Paris just because tradition (or the wedding industry) dictates that, when you both know that you feel more at home in places you know and love: the restaurant where you had your first date, the B&B where you had your first weekend away, or the upper level of the Cusack Stand (if that's your thing). As Chief Wiggum once said: if it feels good, do it.

Buying the Ring

Presenting her with a diamond the size of Rockall on a band of gold may be traditional, especially if the proposal is a surprise, but your idea of a ring and hers may not match, and you only shell out for it once but she's going to have to wear it for the rest of her life. Best leave it to the experts. Let her pick the ring, or at least keep the receipt if you do buy it without her seeing it first. In terms of price, try to spend a month's salary, if you can afford it.

The Stag

Ah, the stag. The bit grooms look forward to most (after the 'I do' part, of course). Things have gone a little crazy on the stag front in Ireland in the last few years. What started off as a few pints out with the lads, as happened in our fathers' time, has turned into a mini-industry that keeps several breweries, airlines and hotels in business. The night out became a weekend away in Wexford, then moved to a weekend in

Prague, and I've even heard of lads going on a week's package holiday in the sun as the latest form of the stag.

Do what you want to do, within reason, and also what you and your mates can afford. You may want to have a long weekend in Prague with the lads from your sports team, another weekend in Kilkenny with the lads from school/work/college and then another booze-soaked night out in your home town, but that all adds up to a lot of expense for those lads, who may be saving for a house, a wedding of their own, or may simply be concerned about their livers.

In my case, I had a mini-stag in Prague with my two oldest friends, though that was five months before the wedding, so it wasn't really a stag, and I also had a weekend in Waterford. Getting away is a good idea, and a foreign trip can be a blast, but choose wisely. Anyone who's been to the Temple Bar area in Dublin on a weekend night can see that all those stag parties of lads from Rotherham, Barnsley and London make the place uncomfortable for the rest of us, especially those of us who live in Dublin. Imagine how the proud citizens of Prague feel when coachloads of lads in GAA jerseys arrive in their city every Friday night for a weekend of cheap booze and not-so-cheap strippers (or so I'm told!).

If you are going away, use your imagination – and cheap flights. Antwerp in Belgium can be reached for around €60 if you play your cards right and it's a good town. Tallin in Estonia has become the new Prague and is infested with English and Scottish stags every weekend, but the same can't be said for lively, fun and inexpensive cities like Bilbao, Bologna, Warsaw, all easily reached by direct (and often cheap) flights from Ireland.

The Rest

Once you've popped the question there isn't a whole lot else for you to do. There are a couple of things you can't leave to her: you'll need a ring, for starters, and a suit.

The buying/rental of the suit for the groomal party, as I like to call it, is remarkably stress-free and as simple as you want it to be. Girls will spend weeks in bridal shops, looking at magazines, scouring the internet, all in the search for that perfect dress. You'll have yourself and your groomal party sorted in less than an hour.

Choose something that makes you feel and look comfortable. There's no point in getting a suit that you hate, just so you can look good in the photos, if you're grimacing in those same photos because you hate the suit you're in.

One friend got married in a regular off-the-rack smart blue suit, with white shirt and red tie, which matched up with his best man and dad's outfits for the day. They all looked comfortable, relaxed and sharp, in a 'Reservoir Dogs' kind of way.

At another wedding the groomal party wore tails, gloves and top hats, which made the father of the groom looked ill at ease and meant he couldn't relax for the whole day. Why add to the profits of Black Tie by renting a top hat, which you don't even wear; you just pose for the photos with the hat in your hand?

Try and take some control here. You don't tell your bride what dress she can wear (you can't even see it beforehand), so she shouldn't make you wear something you don't feel comfortable in. If you really don't want to wear tails, or any form of formal/morning suit, then don't. Wear what you will feel good in. And it doesn't matter all that much what you look like anyway; all eyes will be on the beautiful creature in white beside you.

Why buy a new pair of shoes just for the occasion when you know that your regular black ones are comfortable? After all, you'll be wearing them for around fourteen hours. Another tip: if you do buy a pair of new shoes, make sure you take the price tag off the sole. I didn't. And it was all some people at the ceremony could look at when I was kneeling down.

The Music

Most important part of the day for many grooms. Again, my advice would be to select music that you and your fiancée will like, not what you are expected to have. A jazz band may look great in all those magazines, but do any of your friends really like jazz? I'd rather stuff steel wool in my ears than listen to jazz.

Your choice of music will depend on the venue: some hotels, especially in residential areas, require that the music stop by midnight. At one wedding I attended, the hotel's policy was so strict that no music at all was allowed after 12.30am – not even a sing-song in the residents' bar! Band and DJ is the best combination, if time permits and you can afford it, but it could work just as well to have one of your mates perform as DJ. He'll play the stuff you want and won't insist on playing 'Sweet Caroline' just because it's in the DJ's code of conduct for weddings.

If you're big into music, you could spend hours, even days, worrying about what songs you want to hear and whether all tastes will be catered for. Don't worry too much; you'll spend so much time chatting to long-long relatives and friends at the reception that you won't even hear half the stuff. Do allow yourself a list of three must-play songs, however.

And your first dance is important. Choose wisely. The music at the reception doesn't have to be all about love and happiness (at our wedding everyone danced around happily to the Specials' song 'Too Much Too Young', not caring that the lyrics are about as anti-wedding as could be). But it's probably a good idea to have a romantic song for your first dance, so 'I Used To Love Her But I Had To Kill Her' (Guns 'n' Roses) and 'You're The One For Me, Fatty' (Morrissey) are off the list. So is Hank Williams's 'Wedding Bells', the saddest song ever written.

Go for a song that means a lot to you both, and try something classy and timeless (Beatles, Beach Boys, Scott Walker, Frank Sinatra, Van Morrison, Otis Redding) instead of bland boy bands.

The Big Day

Get a good night's sleep the night before the wedding, but don't go to bed *too* early – you'll never sleep. Have a couple of pints with your best man, dad and close mates. Don't put your shirt on immediately after shaving in the morning – you're a bit nervous now and are bound to have cut yourself. Relax and enjoy your last few hours of single life. Have a pre-match (sorry, pre-wedding) nerve-settler, though maybe not a pint as (a) you'll need a visit to the loo in an hour when you're in the middle of making your vows and (b) it's not the nicest smell off your breath at two o'clock in the afternoon. Make sure your best man gets you to the church nice and early (but not too early) and that he has a good CD or tape in the car (it will ease the nerves). Enjoy saying 'I do'. It's one of the best moments of your life. Enjoy the rest of the day with your guests but remember it's about you and your new wife now, so make sure the pair of you nip off for a couple of minutes on your own every few hours. You will be bought more drinks on this day than any other in your life but you'll be so busy dancing with your wife and talking to your friends you'll drink only a few of them. Don't drink too much; don't go to bed too early or too late.

It's been the best day ever. Make sure you tell her.

CHAPTER FOURTEEN

Final Countdown and the Big Day

The last few weeks before your wedding will be among the scariest, most panic-filled and exciting weeks of your life. All your plans are falling into shape; your hard work is paying off. After months of feeling that no one else realises how important this wedding is, suddenly it seems like everyone is talking about your big day.

As advised in Chapter 2, you will have been using the **Countdown Checklist** on page 284 to keep track of how the various tasks are progressing, but no matter how organised you are, there are lots of jobs which just can't be done until the last few weeks. Here's an outline of what you should be doing in the month before the wedding:

Four weeks to go

If you haven't already done so, finalise the music to be played at the ceremony and who is doing the readings. Get your wedding booklets printed and assembled. This can be time-consuming if you're doing them yourself, so get your bridesmaids or best man to help out.

Start breaking in your shoes by wearing them around the house when your fiancé is out. Scuff the soles on concrete to give you more grip and to make sure you don't slip walking down the highly-polished aisle. Alternatively, you could stick a bit of masking tape to the sole, which also gives more grip.

Have your hair trial. Bring photographs or printouts of any ideas you might have. Bring your tiara or headdress if you're wearing one, and check with the hairdresser whether you should bring your veil – often it's not really necessary. If you don't like the hairstyle, say so; now is not the time for being shy. This is your chance to get it exactly right, and the hairdresser should keep trying different things until you're happy. When you get home take photos of the style from different angles so the hairdresser can match the style exactly on the day, or fix anything you decide you're not happy with.

Have your make-up trial. Again, don't be afraid to speak your mind if there's anything you don't like. Ask someone to take photos so you can see if the make-up looks good on film: you'll be looking at your wedding photos for a long time. If you're doing your own make-up, have a practice run. Leave it on all day to make sure it still looks good in the evening. Your hen party might be a good opportunity to give it a go.

Have your first dress fitting. The dressmaker or sales

boutique will let you know how long any alterations should take.

Hold your hen and stag parties – *see* Chapter 10.

Two weeks to go

Finalise guest numbers. Divide up the task of chasing slow RSVPers – *see* Chapter 9.

Draw up the seating plan – *see* Chapter 12.

Write place cards and divide them up according to table, to save time later. If you have anything else, such as balloons or other decorations for the rooms, table decorations, centrepieces, favours, disposable cameras or a guest book, put them all together in a box ready to take to the hotel.

Have your second dress fitting. Try on your full wedding outfit, including shoes and underwear.

One week to go

Call the photographer to make sure he/she knows what time to arrive at your house or wherever you're staying. If you want to give a list of must-take shots, e-mail or fax it to them now. Confirm how you will be paying (usually a certain percentage on the day or before, and the rest when you get your album).

Call the videographer to confirm what time he/she should arrive and to mention again any particular things you want captured, or any special or unusual plans you have for the ceremony or reception. Confirm how you will be paying (usually a certain percentage on the day or before, and the rest when you get your video/DVD).

Call the cakemaker to confirm when the cake will be dropped off or when you need to collect it. Confirm how you will be paying.

Call the musicians (for both ceremony and reception) to confirm arrangements with them. Confirm how you will be paying.

Call the florist to confirm when the flowers will be dropped off, or if you need to collect them. Confirm whether they need to make a separate delivery to where the men are getting ready. Confirm how you will be paying.

Call the driver to confirm what time he/she should arrive at your house. Confirm how you will be paying.

For any payments that will have to be made on the day, put the correct amount, either cash or cheque, in an envelope, and label it, ready to give to the best man the day before the wedding. This usually includes:

- Priest or other clergy
- Altar servers
- Sacristan, or other church fee
- Organist/choir/church musicians
- Photographer
- Videographer
- Band or DJ
- Driver.

Have a final dress fitting, if necessary. Collect your dress and hang it up carefully. Ask the shop's advice on how best to store it before the wedding: some fabrics are best hung up between two white bedsheets rather than in the protective cover supplied by the shop.

If you're having fake tan applied or your legs waxed, get it done two or three days before the wedding.

Pack for your honeymoon. Put a separate bag together for things you will need the day after the wedding.

Hold the ceremony rehearsal.

Meet with the wedding manager in the hotel to finalise arrangements. Here are some of the areas that you will want to firm up:

- Confirm the time and location of your ceremony so they know when to expect guests to start arriving. If you're hiring a wedding bus, tell them – this means they'll have a large number of guests arriving at once instead of the usual trickle. Find out what the arrangements are for greeting guests when they arrive

- Give them an approximate time that the bride and groom will arrive after having photos taken

- Discuss what time the meal will start

- If you're having your speeches before the meal it's important to let them know, and try to give an estimate of how long the speeches will take, especially if you're having a hot starter

- If you're providing your own decorations (including favours, disposable cameras, place cards etc), when should you deliver them? They may be happy for you to decorate the room yourself the night before as long as there isn't another function there. Otherwise, if the hotel is taking charge of the decorations, give them clear instructions, e.g. number of candles per table, a special decoration for the top table etc

- Give them the number of confirmed guests to date and ask for their cut-off point at which you can no longer make additions or subtractions to that number

- Where will they display the seating plan?

- Are you giving them your own CDs to play during the meal?

- Where is the closest smoking area to the function room?
- If you are bringing flower arrangements on the day (e.g. bringing those used in the church), where can you display them?
- Confirm your menu choices. Give them the number of vegetarian or other special meals required, if they need to know in advance
- If you're supplying your own wine, when can it be delivered to the hotel? When should you collect any leftover bottles?
- How much wine do you want them to open? Should they check with one of you or your parents before going over a certain number?
- How much of the wedding cake should they cut, and how much should they put aside for you? As well as the top tier, you may also want to keep some of the rest of the cake for invited guests or neighbours who couldn't attend
- What time should the band/DJ set up? What time do they have to finish?
- Confirm the time of the evening buffet and what it includes
- What is the situation regarding the residents' bar – does it stay open late and are they very strict about residents only?
- When do they need final payment?

If you are having a venue other than a hotel, you may have additional questions such as when the caterers should set up.

The day before

Try not to leave too many things until the day before so you can have as relaxing a day as possible. Have a manicure (this will take too much time on the morning of the wedding) and any other treatments, such as a pedicure or a massage.

Make sure the men's suits have been picked up from the hire shop.

Entrust the wedding rings to the best man and the wedding booklets to the usher or groomsman.

If you're making a speech, check your notes one last time.

Bring (or get someone to bring) your favours and table decorations, including place cards, to the hotel. Include a few spare place cards, just in case.

If you're having your hair put up, it's usually best to wash it the night before – check with the hairdresser.

Emergency Kit

Put an emergency kit together that will get you through any number of mishaps. If you include everything on this list, it's going to be too big to carry around with you, so plan to leave it in your room if you're staying at the reception venue, in the car, or behind the reception desk.

- Spare tights or stockings. Have two spare pairs, in case you ladder one when putting them on
- Make-up
- Sunglasses
- Headache tablets, and anything else you're inclined to need from time to time, such as indigestion remedies
- Bach Rescue Remedy to keep you calm when you need it most
- Sewing kit for emergency repairs
- Baby wipes to clean any stains off your dress; they work wonders on certain fabrics, but check first that they're suitable for your dress. The shop where you bought the dress should be able to advise
- Mobile phone
- Contact lenses or glasses if you need them
- Copy of your speech

Plan an evening that will be as relaxing as possible. This might mean having the bridesmaids over to watch a film, curling up on the couch with a mug of hot chocolate and having a chat with your mum, having a long relaxing bath scented with lavender oil, or going to the pub with your husband-to-be to enjoy your last night as an engaged couple. It's supposed to be bad luck to see the groom before the ceremony, so make sure you do a Cinderella act and leave before midnight.

If you are a strict Irish traditionalist, now is the time to put the Child of Prague statue in the garden to ensure good weather the next day – my mother did it for me, and it worked!

THE BIG DAY

You'll either be full of anticipation when you wake up – like a child on Christmas morning; completely panic-stricken, thinking about all the things that could go wrong, or just plain lethargic: you've imagined every bit of this day already and it can't possibly be as good as you thought. Well, just wait and see. It's going to be even better.

The important thing is to stay calm and remind yourself that you've prepared everything carefully and you have a whole cast of people making sure that everything goes according to plan. There's nothing you can do now to change things, so just relax and get on with it. Bridemaids or members of your family who are the cool, calm and collected types are the people you need to be with right now; if any of them are making you feel more stressed, don't hesitate to go off for a walk on your own or to ask them to let you be by yourself for a while. And as always, keep the Bach Rescue Remedy close at hand. A glass of champagne or your favourite tipple might help too, but don't overdo it — you don't want red cheeks or overbright eyes spoiling your look, and you definitely don't want to be needing the ladies room when you should be walking down the aisle.

Four hours before the ceremony

Have a light breakfast before you have your hair and make-up done. Wear a shirt or blouse that can be opened at the front so you don't have to pull it over your head.

Have your hair done. Enjoy being transformed into a bride.

Three hours before the ceremony

Have your make-up done. If you're doing it yourself, take your time and ignore anyone hammering on the bathroom door.

The flowers arrive at your home. The best man or other reliable person takes charge of the buttonholes for the men.

Two hours before the ceremony

Have some lunch before you put on your wedding dress. You might not feel hungry now, but you don't want to take the risk of feeling light-headed during the ceremony.

The groom gets dressed.

One hour before the ceremony

The photographer arrives to take photos of you and your bridesmaids getting ready, and photos of you with your parents and family before you leave the house.

Take a minute to look in the mirror and savour the moment — you really are a bride at last!

Half an hour before the ceremony

The groom, best man and groomsmen arrive at the church or registry office. Guests will start to arrive shortly. The florist should be making sure all arrangements are in place, and musicians should be setting up.

The ushers are ready to hand out the wedding booklets as guests arrive and show them to their seats.

The bridesmaids and the bride's mother leave for the church, followed shortly afterwards by the bride and her father. [Obviously, if the journey to the church takes longer than 30 minutes, then the cars will have to leave earlier]

This is a good time to put your engagement ring on your right hand, or give it to your chief bridesmaid to wear for the duration of the ceremony.

The ceremony

All guests are seated and the music has started. The bride's mother is shown to her seat (usually the front pew on the left hand side).

The bride arrives at the church and photographs are taken outside. The entrance music begins and the bride enters. The walk down the aisle is one of the most special parts of the day, but also one of the most nerve-racking. If you're feeling a bit overwhelmed, just focus on the groom waiting for you at the top.

The ceremony will be over quicker than you imagined, and you'll be walking out arm-in-arm as husband and wife.

Leaving the ceremony

The bride and groom and the rest of the bridal party greet the guests as they come out of the church. If you have a big wedding this might be the only time you get to speak to everyone, so enjoy it.

The photographs

The bridal party is whisked away for some photographs, while the guests make their way to the reception.

Tip: Turn your hips slightly to the side – this makes you appear slimmer in photos. Before the wedding, have a look at photos of yourself and see how you look best, for example, smiling with your mouth open or closed, standing at particular angles etc. Close your eyes or look away between shots to help you relax your face and smile more naturally.

The drinks reception

Guests are greeted with champagne/wine/mulled wine/tea and coffee. The bride and groom often miss much of this as they're having photos taken, but don't worry, everyone enjoys the chance to mingle.

The meal

The bride and groom enter the reception room to a standing ovation. They take their seats at the top table and settle down to enjoy their meal.

The speeches

The best man calls for attention and announces the speeches. The speeches should last no more than half an hour.

The entertainment

The musicians/DJ set up. The first dance is announced. Guests gather to watch the bride and groom take to the floor.

The day draws to a close

Weddings used to end with the bride and groom going off to change into going-away outfits, then saying goodbye to their guests before heading off on honeymoon. Now the bride and groom are much more likely to be the last ones standing, singing ballads in the residents' bar with the best of them. If this sounds like you, you can mark the official end of the evening by getting everyone on to the dance floor for the last dance.

Ever notice how time flies when you're enjoying yourself? This is never truer than on your wedding day. You won't believe how quickly the day will go by. One minute you're about to walk down the aisle, the next you're sitting down to dinner, and the intervening hours have just gone by in a whirl. So make sure to savour every minute. Look around at the family and friends who have gathered just for the two of you. All the planning and preparation has been worthwhile; it's all come together at last.

WEDDING DAY CRISES

No matter how well you've planned everything, I've yet to hear about a wedding that didn't have some tiny hitch. What all brides will tell you, though, is that you genuinely don't care on the day. Problems the mere thought of which would have stressed you out a few weeks earlier seem very small in comparison to the fact that you're marrying your true love and you have everyone you care about celebrating with you. Give the phone numbers of all suppliers to someone else, such as your mother or the best man, so you won't have to worry about this.

Here are some of the things that could go wrong, and how to deal with them:

You wake up with a huge spot on your chin

Don't panic. Your make-up artist will be able to cover it almost completely, and spots are never as noticeable to other people as they are to ourselves.

If it happens the day before, you have a bit more time to do something about it. Toothpaste is great for drying out spots, or stick to the old reliables like Dettol.

The weather is horrible

This may seem like a crisis, but believe me, it's not. Of course it would be great if it was a sunny day, but in this country that's a special bonus, not something to count on. You really won't care once the day is under way, and most of the action takes place indoors anyway. Make sure there are plenty of umbrellas to keep you dry between the car and the church and the car and reception; don't walk on the grass as you may get grass stains on your dress, and call the hotel to let them know you'll be having your photos taken there.

Your flowers don't arrive or are the wrong kind

Get your bridesmaid or your mother on the phone to the florist straight away. If they can't sort it out, get on to another florist pronto. If it's too late to get exactly what you wanted, get something very simple such as a small posy of roses. No one will know that isn't what you had planned.

Someone in your bridal party is sick

If they're really too ill to attend, decide whether you should replace them or manage without them. Be sure to keep some cake for them, as well as a few special photos.

You're sick

Dose yourself with painkillers/flu remedies/sickness tablets. Visit the doctor; he or she will do anything they can to make sure you can make it through the day. Put a big smile on your face and battle on. With any luck, adrenaline will carry you through.

There's something wrong with your dress

This really shouldn't happen. You should try on your whole outfit a few days before the wedding and check everything again the day before. If the worst comes to the worst, get the dressmaker to come to your house and do whatever she can to make it work.

The car won't start

It's not the end of the world; the main thing is that you get to the church, not how you get there. Get a neighbour or friend to drive you, and get the ushers to make sure everyone is inside before you arrive. Have someone sort the problem out while the ceremony is on so that there is a replacement car waiting to bring you to the reception.

The traffic is awful

If you are held up, everyone is going to be held up. Check a few days in advance for anything that could cause delays: roadworks, sporting event, fairs etc, and let people know to allow extra time. If you're badly delayed, ring the celebrant and the reception venue to let them know.

A supplier lets you down

There's not much you can do on the day, so just resign yourself to it, and make sure you complain afterwards, reporting them to a consumer organisation or professional association if appropriate.

CHAPTER FIFTEEN

Newly-wed bliss?

You know the expression 'the honeymoon is over'? Well, they invented that for a reason. After the high of the wedding day, many brides come back to earth with a bang. However long you've been planning the wedding, you are sure to feel a sense of anti-climax when it's all over. The day that everyone tells you is the best day of your life is a thing of the past – maybe it can only go downhill from here?

It's only natural to be a bit sad that your big day is over, but focus on the positive. You didn't get married so you could be a star for a day. You got married because you wanted to spend the rest of your life with your new husband, and this is just the beginning.

First things first. There are a few post-wedding jobs that have to be done, and the sooner the better.

Thank-you cards

Make a note of each present you receive as you go along so you'll know what to say in the thank-you cards. Leave space on the list of wedding guests or add a column on your spreadsheet as an easy way of keeping track. You'll probably also receive presents from people you didn't invite to the wedding, such as neighbours of your parents, so don't forget to note those too.

You can either send out your thank-you cards as soon as you receive a present so you'll have less to do after the wedding, or just do them all at once – whatever seems easiest. Try to get them done within three or four months of the wedding, otherwise you'll probably have some of your guests complaining that the standards of today's youth are slipping! Etiquette says that wedding presents can be given up to a year after the wedding, so don't be surprised if there are a few late ones.

You can order your thank-you cards at the same time as the rest of your wedding stationery, make them yourself, or buy packets from card shops. A popular choice for making your own is to print a wedding photo on the cards. Alternatively, some photographers will give you tiny snapshots of your favourite wedding photo, which you can slip in with the cards. These make a lovely souvenir for those who attended the wedding, and give those who couldn't make it a chance to see how the bride and groom looked.

Decide how you're going to divide up the job of writing the cards. The bride often gets landed with the whole lot, but if you plan to share tasks equally in your household then start as you mean to go on! You could each write the cards to your own relatives and friends, or swap lists and use the opportunity to communicate with the other side of your new family.

Write something personal on each card, mentioning the gift. For example:

Dear Mary,
Thank you very much for the lovely vase. It looks great in our sitting room.
   or
We really appreciate your kind gift of the duvet set. It matches our bedroom perfectly.

Where a gift has come from the wedding list you drew up, you may feel that you can't compliment the giver's choice since you picked it out! In this case you could say something like:

Thank you very much for the cutlery set. It was great to get exactly what we wanted!

For guests who attended your wedding, it's nice to acknowledge their presence as well as their presents:

Thanks too for sharing in our wedding day; it made it all the more special having you there.

Writing thank-you cards is not a very exciting job and you'll feel like you're repeating yourself *ad nauseum* by the time you get to number 52, but people really do appreciate them, so it's worth taking the time.

Ordering your album

You should get proofs from the photographer within a few weeks of your wedding, from which you select the photos you want for your album. Set aside an evening to make your choices together and try to get it out of the way early; it becomes more of a chore the longer you put it off (I speak from personal experience here!) and some photographers will charge you extra if you don't get it done within a certain timeframe.

When choosing your photos, have a good mixture of posed shots and 'story' type shots showing the different stages of the day.

Don't worry about ordering individual prints; you can do that later. Sometimes it helps to see your album first to decide which you like best.

Saving your wedding mementos

You'll probably have lots of bits and pieces you want to save, such as wedding candles, the ornament from the top of the cake, your garter – the list can be as long as you like, really. You can get lovely wedding keepsake boxes from card shops or stores like Debenhams or Marks and Spencer. For a cheaper option just get an ordinary box and decorate it yourself. It's probably best to store this out of sight in the attic or on top of a wardrobe rather than on your coffee table, in case your less romantic friends might think you're a bit sad!

Some brides decide to have their wedding bouquets preserved and framed. For some reason this has always struck me as slightly macabre, but maybe that's just me. If you'd like to do it and don't know how to go about it, ask your florist for a recommendation. Give your bridesmaid or a trusted friend the task of getting the bouquet to them the day after the wedding.

What do you do with your dress?

Get your wedding dress cleaned as soon as you can, before stains have a chance to discolour the fabric permanently. If possible, get someone to look after this job for you while you're on honeymoon. Most wedding dresses are best dry cleaned, though I do know one bride whose mother washed her dress by hand in the bath; it turned out fine but I'm not sure I would take the risk!

Deciding what to do with your dress is the next dilemma. If you're the sentimental type you'll probably want to keep it, maybe in the hope that your daughter will wear it one day. Another nice tradition is to have it made into a christening robe or First Communion dress.

You may decide to sell it to recoup some of the cost. Call the shop where you bought it to see if they'll take it off your hands. If they don't sell secondhand dresses, they may be able to recommend someone who does. You could also sell it yourself by putting an ad in the local paper, posting on a weddings website or even selling it on eBay. Set a realistic price: you are unlikely to get more than a third to a half of what you paid for it.

If you decide to keep your dress, you'll need to store it properly so it doesn't decay. The best way to store it is in an acid-free box. You can buy them from drycleaners or order online from websites such as www.emptybox.co.uk. Store the box in a cool dry place away from direct sunlight.

What do you do with your accessories?

Veils, tiaras and headdresses are easier (both practically- and sentimentally-speaking) to sell on or lend to another bride. If you're keeping yours you can store them with your dress.

As for your shoes, bridal shoes can usually be dyed another colour. Consult with a shoe repair shop and see if you can get them dyed to match a special outfit – you might even get to wear them to another wedding.

What do you do with the bridesmaid dresses?

If the dresses were deliberately chosen with a view to being wearable at dances and other functions, then the bridesmaids will get some use out of them again. But it's a bit of a waste if the dresses are going to be left hanging in wardrobes, never to be worn again. If you paid for the dresses you're entitled to tell the girls you'd like to sell them on after the wedding. (You should definitely make this part of the deal if they try to talk you into buying dresses that are more expensive than you had budgeted for!)

Bridesmaid dresses are often easier to sell secondhand than wedding dresses. One kind bride I know decided to sell the bridesmaid dresses and used the proceeds to treat them all to a night out.

WHAT'S IN A NAME?

Will you change your name?

I discovered that people have very strong opinions on what is the correct thing to do, and, unfortunately, they won't be at all reluctant to tell you what that is. So, unless you are lucky enough to know instinctively which decision is right for you, you are likely to sway violently from one to the other (just like on your hen night after too many tequilas, in fact). You will find your feminist principles at war with the newfound affection for all things traditional that so many brides develop.

Your mother-in-law may be horrified if you plan to keep your own name, your single friends will be shocked if you don't, while your darling husband will tell you to make up your own mind, while possibly secretly feeling hurt that you are experiencing any misgivings about becoming Mrs X.

Reasons to keep your maiden name:

♥ You feel strongly that your name is part of your identity

♥ You are well known in your business or profession

♥ It's more important to you that people identify you with your family of origin than with your husband

♥ He has a horrible name which doesn't go with yours!

Reasons to change your name:

♥ You want people to know immediately that you're married

♥ You want to have the same surname as your children

♥ It avoids confusion in the long term

♥ You want to wipe out your terrible credit history and start again

♥ You have a horrible surname that you've been dying to get rid of!

Of course it's not simply an 'either or' choice. You could:

♥ Use both names. This is a very popular option chosen by many women, most commonly by keeping their maiden names for work, and using their married names socially

♥ Go double-barrelled. This works well with some names, though it can be seen as pretentious, and with longer names it can just be plain ridiculous.

♥ Keep your own name until you have children, then decide if you want to change.

Another possibility is that your husband could decide to take your name instead, or the two of you could be really modern and choose a new surname together, perhaps made up of a combination of your names. Both these options will require your husband to change his name by deed poll (with the second option, you won't have to change yours by deed poll if he changes his before the wedding).

Francis Skeffington, a journalist, pacifist and campaigner for women's rights, was so committed to equality that when he married Hanna Sheehy in 1903, he added his wife's surname to his own. The couple then used Sheehy Skeffington as their surname. They later founded the Irish Women's Franchise League. Francis was arrested by the British authorities during the 1916 Rising, although he was not involved in the activities, and was shot without trial.

Whatever you decide, you are not going to please everyone. Just remember that it is your name and your decision. If you are challenged – by one side or the other – here are some suggested responses:

If you are changing your name:

The surname you have now is (in most cases) your father's surname. It has been passed down through the male line and reflects nothing of the marvellous women who have played their part in making the wonderful creature that is you. So why should it be any more sexist to take your husband's name than your father's?

If you're not:

You already have a name and you are happy with it. Open your eyes wide with wonder when you say this, as if your questioner had assumed you struggled through life surnameless up until now.

Notification of change of name:

Passport Office
Tax Office
Motor Tax Office (to change your driving licence)
Electoral register
Bank
Insurance Company
Mortgage Provider
Doctor
Dentist
Accountant
Mobile phone bill
Home phone bill
Electricity bill
Gas bill

To change your passport and driving licence, you'll need the original marriage certificate. The passport office now charge you the full price of a new passport to change your name. For banks, a legal photocopy will do. (This is a photocopy made in a solicitor's office and given their stamp). For bills etc, most companies will just take your word for it and change it for you over the phone.

Here is a sample letter to banks, building societies etc.

Bank account no:

Dear Sir or Madam,

Following my marriage on 16th May 2005, I would like to change my bank account in the name of Lily Byrne into my married name, Lily O'Donnell. I enclose a registered copy of my marriage certificate; please return this.

Yours faithfully,

Lily O'Donnell (be sure to sign in your married name).

APPLYING FOR YOUR MARRIAGE CERT

You apply for your marriage certificate to the same Registrar of Births, Marriages and Deaths where you sent the notification of your intention to marry. You can ring the office, write them a letter, or fill in a form printed out from their website. They charge a fee for the certificate: €6.98 at the time of writing.

The marriage certificate does not give your married name; it states that Lily Byrne married Neil O'Donnell on 16th May 2005. The effect of this is that Lily is entitled to use the surname O'Donnell from that date if she so wishes.

If you get married in a church, the celebrant will send you out a church certificate, or may even give it to you on the day.

This is not the same as the civil marriage certificate; you still need to apply for the latter in order to be able to change your name on legal documents.

TAX OPTIONS FOR MARRIED COUPLES

You need to inform the tax office of your marriage, giving the date and both your PPS numbers.

In the year of your marriage, both of you will continue to be taxed as two single persons. However, if you would have paid less tax as a married couple, at the end of the year you can claim a refund of the difference for the months after the marriage took place.

In the following years, you have three options for taxation as a married couple: joint assessment, separate assessment, or you can both continue to be assessed as single people.

Assessment as a single person

This means that each of you is treated as a single person, so:

- Each of you is taxed on your individual income
- Both get the tax credits and the same standard rate cut-off point as a single person
- Each pays your own tax
- You cannot transfer tax credits or standard rate cut-off point to each other.

You need to write to your tax office to claim assessment as a single person. You must apply within the tax year, ideally at the beginning of the year in January. With this option, each of you is responsible for your own tax return.

In some circumstances, this is an unfavourable option, mainly due to the fact that you can't transfer unused tax credits.

Separate assessment

This means that your tax affairs are independent of each other. However, unlike assessment as a single person, some tax credits are divided equally between you. These are: the married tax credit, age tax credit, blind person's tax credit and incapacitated child tax credit. The tax credits are divided up in proportion to the cost borne by you. Any tax credits (other than the PAYE tax credit and employment expenses) that one partner doesn't use can be claimed by the other.

In order to claim separate assessment, you need to write to your tax office between 1 October and 31 March. This option can't be backdated, and it remains in force until one of you informs the tax office in writing that you wish to change it.

With this option, each of you can complete a separate return of your own income, or you can make a joint return.

Joint assessment

This is usually the most favourable option for a married couple, particularly when one of you earns a higher salary. It means that the tax credits and standard rate cut-off point can be shared between you in whatever way suits your circumstances. If you want to go for this option you don't need to inform the tax office in writing, as they will automatically give it to you when you advise them of your marriage.

If only one of you has taxable income, that person will receive all the tax credits and standard rate cut-off point.

If you both have taxable incomes, you can decide which of you is to be the assessable partner, and ask the tax office to allocate the tax credits and standard rate cut-off point in whatever way suits you. PAYE tax credits, employment expenses and the basic standard rate cut-off point are not transferable.

You can decide between you who is to be the assessable spouse, and how you want to divide up the credits etc. The assessable spouse must complete the return of income for both of you.

If you don't nominate an assessable spouse, the tax office will automatically treat the person with the highest income as the assessable spouse. If you don't specify how you want the tax credits divided up, the tax office will normally give all the tax credits (other than the other person's PAYE and employment expense credits) to the assessable spouse.

The person who becomes the assessable spouse remains as such until you both decide the other one should be the assessable spouse, or until one of you opts for separate assessment or assessment as a single person.

You can get a form from your local tax office, or print it off from their website, which you complete to nominate one of you as the assessable spouse and to state how you wish to divide up your tax credits. The tax office should also be able to help with any questions you have regarding your options. For more information *see* www.revenue.ie.

COPING WITH POST-NUPTIAL DEPRESSION

It's an unfortunate reality that the high of your wedding day often doesn't last very long. Almost as soon as the next day you could wake up feeling crushed that your big day is over and wishing you could do it all again. You begin to wonder if there's something wrong with you. You've just married the most wonderful man you've ever met, so shouldn't you be happy to be married instead of longing to be a bride-to-be again?

Relax, you're normal; you've just got a case of post-nuptial depression. Symptoms include the following:

- ♥ You wonder what on earth you're going to do with yourself in the evenings and at weekends when you don't have plans to make or dresses to try on
- ♥ You agonise over tiny things that went wrong on the wedding day and wonder if you should have done things differently
- ♥ You feel jealous of friends who still have their big day before them
- ♥ You want to take over the weddings of said friends because you just know you can organise it better than they can
- ♥ You feel that you have nothing to look forward to and nothing nice is ever going to happen again.

Luckily, the treatment for this condition is quite nice, really. First of all, plan something special for yourself and your new husband to look forward to. A holiday or a long weekend a few months after the wedding is the perfect antidote to post-wedding blues.

Rejoice in the fact that, while on an everyday level not much has changed in your relationship, you do have a nice warm sense of security and closeness, which was probably not as strong before. Other people will also see you differently; you're a family now and your relatives and friends will take it for granted that you'll put each other first. That's once they get over boring you to death by asking if your relationship has changed (Gosh, would you believe you're the first person to ask me that!).

Don't interfere with other people's wedding plans or insist on offering advice unless asked. You probably thought you knew it all before *your* big day and wished other ex-brides would just let you get on with it. Now you're older and wiser, but you have to let other people go through this process for themselves. By all means be ready to share the wisdom of your experience if people ask. You're bound to have recommendations about suppliers that are invaluable to future brides, but accept that not everyone wants to do things the same way as you.

Take advantage of the extra time and money you have now that planning and saving for the wedding are a thing of the past. Take up an evening class or a new hobby. Throw yourself into redecorating your house or apartment; this is always a fun project and the best bit is that it is never really finished.

Do like I did: write a book! Believe me, you will be too busy to be depressed.

THE BABY QUESTION

What!! Yes, unless you already have children, you'll hardly be back down the aisle before people start asking you when you're planning to start a family. If you're not intending to have children for a few years (or at all) this can be really irritating. If you're trying to conceive right away it can be even worse; if you get pregnant quickly you probably won't want to tell anyone until the first three months have passed, and if you have trouble conceiving, nosy questions can be very upsetting. Try telling people that your biological clock isn't ticking just yet as you've taken the batteries out. Or be really blunt and say 'We'll wait and see what happens – while we're on the subject, how's your sex life?' – that should soon shut them up.

LOOKING TO THE FUTURE

You have realised one dream: you've married the man you love and who loves you. Now it's time to get on with all the other dreams. And with the organisational, diplomatic and motivational skills you have acquired in planning your wonderful wedding, it should be no bother to you!

I wish you continued joy and success.

COUNTDOWN CHECKLIST

This timeframe assumes that your wedding day is at least 12 months away. If your big day is sooner than this, you can compress some of early stages into one.

As soon as you get engaged
☐ Decide what style of wedding you will have
☐ Decide approximately how many guests you will invite
☐ Set a date for the wedding (with alternative options, to allow for availability of venues)
☐ Draw up a rough budget, decide who pays for what, and start saving

One year to go
☐ Choose a church or registry office, meet the celebrant and book the date
☐ Book your reception venue
☐ Choose your bridal party
☐ Draw up an initial guest list
☐ Book a photographer

Nine months to go
☐ Book a videographer
☐ Book a band and/or DJ
☐ Start looking for your dress

Six months to go

- [ ] Order your dress
- [ ] Order your veil and headdress
- [ ] Decide on bridesmaids' dresses
- [ ] Book your florist
- [ ] Order your wedding cake
- [ ] Finalise your guest list, after discussion with both sets of parents
- [ ] Order invitations and other stationery
- [ ] Book musicians or singers for ceremony
- [ ] Choose music and readings for ceremony
- [ ] Book wedding cars/bus
- [ ] Book wedding night accommodation for the bride and groom
- [ ] Book your honeymoon
- [ ] Start thinking about where you would like to have your gift list

Four months to go

- [ ] Buy shoes
- [ ] Decide on accessories for bridesmaids
- [ ] Choose suits for the groom, best man and other leading men
- [ ] Choose your wedding rings
- [ ] Check that your passport is up to date
- [ ] Get inoculations for honeymoon, if necessary

☐ Send notification of intention to marry (must be done no less than three months before the day)

☐ Meet the celebrant to discuss your music and readings

Three months to go

☐ Book hair and make-up appointments

☐ Register for a gift list

☐ Ask relatives or friends to read at the ceremony

Two months to go

☐ Send out your invitations

☐ Buy thank-you presents for parents and bridal party

☐ Meet your florist to choose flowers

☐ Arrange dress fittings

☐ Finalise wedding booklet

☐ Decide on going-away or next-day outfit

One month to go

☐ Have dress fittings

☐ Get wedding booklets printed

☐ Have hair and make-up trials

☐ Hold hen and stag parties

☐ Break in your wedding shoes

Two weeks to go

☐ Finalise guest numbers and draw up seating plan

☐ Try on full wedding outfit including shoes and underwear

☐ Arrange for any alterations that may be necessary

One week to go

☐ Hold rehearsal

☐ Confirm arrangements for reception

☐ Confirm arrangements for the photographer, videographer, cake, musicians, driver, florist

☐ Collect your dress

☐ Pack for your honeymoon

The day before

☐ Deliver favours or table decorations to the hotel

☐ Leave your luggage for the day after the wedding at the hotel

☐ Put your emergency kit together

☐ Have a manicure

☐ Keep your fingers crossed for good weather!

BUDGET PLANNER

BRIDE

ITEM	ESTIMATED COST €	ACTUAL COST €
Ring		
Dress		
Veil		
Headdress or Tiara		
Shoes		
Underwear		
Hair styling		
Make-up		
Nails		
Facials/Tanning/Waxing		
Jewellery		
Going-Away/Next Day Outfit & accessories		
Other		
Sub-total:		

GROOM

ITEM	ESTIMATED COST €	ACTUAL COST €
Ring		
Suit (Hire or purchase)		
Shoes		
Accessories (shirt, tie etc)		
Going-Away/Next Day Outfit & accessories		
Other		
Sub-total:		

BRIDESMAID(S)

ITEM	ESTIMATED COST €	ACTUAL COST €
Dress		
Shoes		
Accessories		
Hair		
Make-up		
Other		
Sub-total:		

BEST MAN/GROOMSMEN

ITEM	ESTIMATED COST €	ACTUAL COST €
Suit hire		
Sub-total:		

FLOWER GIRLS, PAGE BOYS

ITEM	ESTIMATED COST €	ACTUAL COST €
Dress		
Suit		
Accessories		
Other		
Sub-total:		

FLOWERS

ITEM	ESTIMATED COST €	ACTUAL COST €
Bouquets		
Buttonholes and corsages		
Church / Registry Office Flowers		
Reception Flowers		
Sub-total:		

TRANSPORT

ITEM	ESTIMATED COST €	ACTUAL COST €
Wedding car/cars		
Wedding Bus		
Other		
Sub-total:		

STATIONERY

ITEM	ESTIMATED COST €	ACTUAL COST €
Wedding Invitations		
Inserts (RSVP cards/Accommodation listing, etc)		
Postage		
Wedding Booklets		
Thank-You Cards		
Place cards/menus		
Other		
Sub-total:		

PHOTOGRAPHY

ITEM	ESTIMATED COST €	ACTUAL COST €
Photographer (incl wedding album)		
Videographer		
Extra Prints/Small albums		
Disposable cameras for guest tables		
Developing Charges		
Other		
Sub-total:		

CAKE

ITEM	ESTIMATED COST €	ACTUAL COST €
Cake		
Cake Stands and Tiers (unless provided by venue)		
Delivery Charge		
Other		
Sub-total:		

CEREMONY

ITEM	ESTIMATED COST €	ACTUAL COST €
Celebrant's fee		
Altar servers/Sacristan/Other		
Singer(s)		
Organist/musicians		
Other		
Sub-total:		

RECEPTION

ITEM	ESTIMATED COST €	ACTUAL COST €
Venue Hire		
Food		
Wine		
Drinks reception on arrival		
Champagne/Sparkling wine for toast		
Corkage (if providing own wine)		
Bridal Suite		
Table Decorations		
Favours		

ITEM	ESTIMATED COST €	ACTUAL COST €
Other		
Sub-total:		

RECEPTION MUSIC

ITEM	ESTIMATED COST €	ACTUAL COST €
Band		
DJ		
Other		
Sub-total:		

GIFTS

ITEM	ESTIMATED COST €	ACTUAL COST €
Bridesmaids		
Best Man and Groomsmen		
Mother of Bride		
Mother of Groom		
Other		
Sub-total:		

MISCELLANEOUS

ITEM	ESTIMATED COST €	ACTUAL COST €
Confetti/petals/bubbles		
Press Engagement/Wedding announcements		
Rehearsal Dinner		
Sub-total:		

HONEYMOON

ITEM	ESTIMATED COST €	ACTUAL COST €
Travel		
Accommodation		
Insurance		
Spending Money		
Passports		
Visas		
Vaccinations		
Other		
Sub-total:		

TOTALS

Item	Estimated Cost €	Actual Cost €
Bride		
Groom		
Bridesmaid(s)		
Best man/Groomsmen		
Flower girls, page boys		
Flowers		
Transport		
Stationery		
Photography		
Cake		
Ceremony		
Reception		
Reception Music		
Gifts		
Miscellaneous		
Honeymoon		
Grand total:		

USEFUL WEBSITES

Below are some websites that I and the other brides I talked to found useful when planning our weddings. It's not an exhaustive list, nor is it an endorsement of these websites, as by their nature websites can and do change frequently. So feel free to pick and choose and explore at random!

www.weddingsonline.ie and www.simplyweddings.ie are two of the best general weddings websites in Ireland. You'll find lots of useful articles and advice on both sites, but best of all are the discussion forums, where you can swap stories and advice with other brides-to-be.

www.gettingmarried.ie, a Catholic Church website, is very useful in planning your church ceremony.

www.ezweddingplanner.com features free web-based software for wedding planning, including budgeting, guest lists and e-mail reminders.

www.hitched.co.uk is great for readings, has a huge selection of sample speeches, and also has a discussion forum.

www.confetti.co.uk also has lots of readings, as well as a great selection of favours, decorations and gifts.

www.oasis.gov.ie has a section dedicated to legal aspects of getting married in the Republic of Ireland.

www.groni.gov.uk has the equivalent information for Northern Ireland.

www.groireland.ie is the place to go for the latest news on the implementation of the reform of the marriage laws.

www.gownsales.com and www.bridesave.com sell discount bridal and bridesmaid dresses from the US.

www.irishphotographers.com is the website of the Irish Professional Photographers Association – useful for finding a photographer in your area.

www.cakesandfavours.com is great for ordering favours and decorations, whether readymade or materials for DIY.

www.webwedding.co.uk/articles/music lets you listen to music online.

www.theknot.com and www.marthastewart.com have lots of interesting sections but the wedding bouquet galleries are particularly useful.

INDEX